MASTERING FEAR

MASTERING FEAR

FEAR

A NAVY SEAL'S GUIDE

BRANDON WEBB
and JOHN DAVID MANN

PORTFOLIO / PENGUIN

Portfolio/Penguin
An imprint of Penguin Random House LLC
375 Hudson Street
New York, New York 10014

Most Portfolio books are available at a discount when purchased in quantity
for sales promotions or corporate use. Special editions, which include personalized covers, excerpts, and corporate imprints, can be created when purchased in large quantities. For more information, please call (212) 572-2232 or
e-mail specialmarkets@penguinrandomhouse.com. Your local bookstore can
also assist with discounted bulk purchases using the Penguin Random House
corporate Business-to-Business program. For assistance in locating a participating retailer, e-mail B2B@penguinrandomhouse.com.

ISBN 9780525533566 (hardcover)
ISBN 9780525533573 (ebook)

Printed in the United States of America
10 9 8 7 6 5 4 3 2 1

Book design by Tiffany Estreicher

CONTENTS

*To all those who have the courage to look fear
in the eye and take the next step*

MASTERING FEAR

INTRODUCTION

IN THE POOL

The brave man is not the one who has no fear,
he is the one who triumphs over his fear.
—Nelson Mandela

M Y FRIEND KAMAL is a world traveler; he has meditated with Tibetan monks in the Dalai Lama's monastery, trekked the Himalayas, and hiked the Camino de Santiago in Spain. He served in the U.S. Army and studied to be an ER doctor. He has launched tech companies, runs his own venture capital firm, and is a bestselling author. In person, he makes quite the striking impression: flowing mane of silver hair, quiet voice behind steely gaze, the super-calm demeanor of a Buddhist master. Here is a guy with all the ingredients for success on a mega scale. But I recently learned a secret about Kamal.

He couldn't swim.

At first I had a hard time believing it. I thought he had to be exaggerating. To me, swimming comes as naturally as breathing. I grew up on and in the water. My family lived for years on a sailboat. I spent more than a decade in the navy, trained and deployed as a U.S. Navy SEAL. The idea of not knowing how to swim was beyond my comprehension. But here was my friend, this amazing, talented guy who had accomplished so much in his life . . . and *he couldn't swim.*

I gave him kind of a hard time about it. I pointed out that the human body is more than 60 percent water; did he realize he was already floating around inside his own skin? I wondered aloud if, when his parents conceived him, the egg cell had to swim down to meet the sperm cells, instead of the other way around.

"Dude," I said. "How can you possibly not know how to swim?"

The answer was simple.

Fear.

Kamal had been terrified of water his whole life, he told me. A few times, when he was living in the Dominican Republic, he went kitesurfing. He always wore a life jacket, but that didn't make any difference. He was still terrified. What would happen if he fell and hit the water? He told me stories about being out at his buddy Tim Ferriss's house in the Hamptons. Tim has a big, beautiful pool in his backyard where people hang out and go swimming and have a fantastic time, and Kamal felt awful that he could never join in.

Kamal, I realized, *hated* the fact that he couldn't swim. And it wasn't as if he'd never tried to learn. He'd taken courses, studied in online workshops. For a while he lived in a building in San Francisco with the only heated outdoor Olympic pool in the city, and he brought in a private instructor. That hadn't worked, either. No matter what the various teachers tried, he couldn't handle the feeling of his feet not touching the bottom, and he would quickly reach the point of panic. Now he was thinking about doing one of those immersion courses in Florida. Or so he said. But I noticed he kept putting it off.

I stopped giving him a hard time about it.

Instead, I decided to do something about it.

I had a week coming up at home in New York. "Look," I said. "You give me a commitment for a week, and I'll teach you myself. But you have to commit to meet me, every day at the same time, rain or shine. Give me a week, and I'll have you swimming."

"Okay," he said.

On the appointed morning, I went into the New York Athletic Club, right off Central Park South, headed upstairs to the pool, found a free lane, and slipped into the water. I got there a little early so I could take some laps while I waited for Kamal. As I shot silently up the lane, my thoughts slipstreamed back two decades.

IT'S NIGHTTIME OVER the Persian Gulf, summer of 1995. The four of us—pilot, copilot, another crewman, and me—have been out in our H-60 Seahawk helicopter doing sonar ops. It's been a long night, and we need to refuel on a nearby destroyer before heading back to the aircraft carrier we're calling home.

The pilot slows us down to a crawl as we approach the vessel below. Landing on a destroyer's deck is always dicey, more so on this moonless night. Someone needs to spot the deck as we hover in place high above the ship and talk the pilot down. Tonight the spotter, the guy strapped into the gunner's seat down in the belly of the bird, is me.

I crack open the door and look down, scanning for telltale lights. There aren't any. That's weird. I glance upward—and *now* I see lights. *What?* For the span of a single breath, I experience total disorientation. Why are there lights up here at eye level when the destroyer is way down below us? Then the disorientation evaporates as I look down again and see water, right there at my feet. Persian Gulf water—churning, grinning, reaching up for me, curling around my ankles.

Oh, shit.

We're not hovering high above the ship after all. Our goddamn pilot has put us right down in the drink. Seawater is pouring into the cabin, caressing my legs, climbing the interior walls, searching for the engine. *Hey, baby. I'm here. Come to Papa.* This is not good. If the engine chokes and dies, we flip upside down, sink straight to the bottom of the Gulf, and don't come up again. Ever.

"Altitude!" I shout into my comms. "Altitude!"

And here's where it really starts to get fun. Because our pilot, the guy in charge of this operation, the guy who's supposed to be our leader, is now seized by full-on panic—and he freezes. *"What's happening?"* he screams as he takes exactly zero corrective action. *"Oh God oh God oh God . . . !"* This is not what you want to hear from your helicopter commander in a moment like this. Fear has paralyzed him, taken him, swallowed him whole.

And because of that, all four of us are going to die, right here, right now.

I FINISHED MY laps and pulled myself back up onto the pool's edge to wait for my friend.

I knew what it was that had Kamal in its grip. And I knew why all those other teachers who'd tried to help him had failed. They thought they were supposed to teach him how to swim. They were wrong. This wasn't about learning how to swim.

It was about learning how to harness fear.

During SEAL training there's a pool competency phase where the instructors do everything they can to freak you out. They send you down with an oxygen tank and then tie your air hose in knots so it doesn't work, anything to throw you into a panic, and then see if you can find your way out. You sit there, waiting for your turn with your back to the pool, and listen to the classmate ahead of you in the water, thrashing and drowning. It never got to me, but it sure terrified the living crap out of quite a few classmates. And I could understand why. I might not be afraid of the water normally, but I just about shit my pants that night over the Gulf.

We didn't die, though, for one reason: our copilot, Kennedy, knew how to harness fear. He ignored our useless gibbering pilot and commandeered the controls himself, pulling us up out of the water and planting us safely on the destroyer's deck. To this day I don't know how he did it. It should have been impossible. (The maintenance chief thought we were making the whole thing up until his crew undid the tail section and ten gallons of seawater poured out.) But fear like that will let you do impossible things—if you know how to channel it.

Kennedy knew how to channel it, and it's a good thing he did. If he hadn't, you wouldn't be reading these pages, because I wouldn't be here.

As I said, I grew up on the water. Love it, spent my childhood in it, and a good chunk of my adulthood, too. But there's a reason people use water when they want to drive you to the edge of sanity and break your spirit. If I say, "I'm going to drape a cloth over your mouth and soak it with water," that doesn't sound too bad, does it? Oh, but it is. It can push strong-willed men right over the edge. In my military training I got familiar with the process of waterboarding: in essence, you are slowly, methodically being drowned to death, engulfed by water. There is something primal about the terror this touches.

When I was a kid, I saw a girl drown because of someone's carelessness. I was there when they brought her body up and laid her out on the deck, statue-still, never to take another breath. It was the first time I'd seen death, up close, ugly, and personal. I'll never forget it.

I've seen death take others, too, many times since then, including some close friends. Including my *best* friend. And I've seen other deaths as well—my first business going up in smoke and taking my life savings with it, the dissolution of my marriage, projects that didn't work out, friendships lost, the death of ego and dreams.

Yes, I understood why my friend was afraid.

A few minutes later, Kamal showed up. Right on time. We sat at the pool's edge, our legs in the water. I pushed off and slipped down under. He followed, lowering himself in slow and tense, hands gripping the lip of the wall. He'd never been in a ten-foot depth before. "I'm in," he murmured, but his body language was screaming, *and there's no way in hell I'm letting go of this wall!*

We got to work.

That first day I kept things light. Nice and easy, almost too easy.

The second day we repeated everything we did the first day and went a little further.

The third day he did ten laps on his back.

"You're swimming, man," I told him. He was startled to realize that it was true.

On day four, instead of sitting down poolside and carefully slipping into the water, he went running to the edge, launched himself in the air, and landed in the pool in a humongous cannonball. Huge splash, water everywhere—and then Kamal's face bobbing up in the middle of it, grinning like a kid.

He had never done a cannonball before in his life.

And that's how every lesson started for the rest of the week: Kamal running to the edge, jumping off, and doing a giant cannonball into the pool, then surfacing with that Cheshire Cat grin. A big, grown-up, silver-haired kid. I'd never seen anyone so happy in my life.

On that third day, the day he did ten laps on his back and I told him, "You're swimming, man," and he realized that it was true, we had an interesting conversation at the end of the lesson.

"You know, other people have tried to teach me," he said, "but it never took. They would get me in the water, demonstrate a stroke, and then get impatient when I couldn't do it. They would get frustrated and say, 'It's so easy, man, just *try* it.' But I couldn't 'just try it.' I was too terrified." He looked out across the pool.

"Until now," I said.

Still looking at the water, he nodded. "Yeah. Until now."

Then he looked back at me and said, "You need to write a book about this."

So here it is.

In the following pages, I'm going to show you exactly what I did with Kamal, why it worked, and how you can do it, too.

I'm going to show you how you can do what our copilot Kennedy did that night over the Gulf, and pull yourself through even the most terrifying circumstances.

I'm going to help you master your fear.

In other words: to master your *life*.

THE BATTLE IS IN YOUR MIND

Fear is one of the best friends a champion has.

—JOSÉ TORRES,
world light heavyweight champion

THE THREE OF us are picking through the desert hard-scrabble, collecting the packs another platoon stashed here earlier, when we hear a sound. We turn and look up the ravine toward the dirt road where we parked our truck a few minutes ago. A crowd of maybe fifty Afghan guys is standing up there, seven or eight yards away, looking down at us. A crowd of Afghan guys with guns. A crowd of Afghan guys with guns, who don't look happy.

It's early 2002, just a few months after 9/11, and we are in northeastern Afghanistan on a search-and-seizure operation, looking for bad guys. We wonder if maybe we just found some.

We wonder if maybe some just found us.

Now they're moving closer.

Now they've surrounded us. A few have hung back by our truck, and there's nothing in the sweet wide world stopping them from climbing in and driving it away, leaving us stranded with their armed and very pissed-off friends.

I feel something shifting inside. Certain blood vessels constrict, others dilate. My palms suddenly feel cool, yet moist with sweat. Tiny hairs on the backs of my arms and neck stand at attention. My mouth is dry, my hearing suddenly more acute. I can practically feel the release and surge of epinephrine as my adrenals fire off their liquid torpedoes. *Fire one! One's away, sir! Fire two!* My face doesn't show it, but in my mind, I smile. I know what this is.

This is fear. And I'm about to *use* it.

There's no time to assess or strategize. This is going down, right now. The handful by the truck have the high ground—always a tactical advantage in any armed conflict—and the rest have us immobilized here in the ravine. There are three of us, four or five dozen of them. They outnumber and outgun us in every possible way. Physically, logistically speaking, there is no way for us to prevail here. We'll have to do it through sheer balls and bravado.

We shout at them, yell aggressive words we know they don't understand. They scream back words we don't know, either.

They push closer. Now they're physically shoving us.

Our nerve ends are blazing electrochemical fireworks,

adrenals and pituitaries lighting up our brain stems and spinal nerves with the buzz of a million years of struggle and survival. The air around us crackles. We shout louder.

They don't flinch.

We get right up in their faces, as if *we* were the ones with the upper hand here. We brandish our weapons. If this were a cowboy movie we would fire shots into the ground at their feet, too, only this isn't a movie and we aren't John Wayne and we are *not* fucking around here and they know it. If we shoot, it won't be into the ground.

They stop coming closer. They start backing off.

We hightail our balls and bravado up the ravine and into the truck and back to our camp, our heartbeats gradually slowing back to normal as we bump along the dirt road. Were we afraid? You bet your ass we were.

That was what *saved* us.

You've done this. I know you have. You wouldn't be here, reading this, if you hadn't.

No, you probably have not faced down a group of heavily armed hostile fighters on foreign soil. But at some point in your life you've faced down threatening people or situations, in ways big or small. Everyone has. It's part of the human condition.

There have been moments when your fear caused you to

mobilize, to tap some inner strength or ability and go beyond where you thought you could go. And no doubt, there have also been times when fear made you back down and back out. Like I said: the human condition.

Before you read on, I want you to think about this for a moment, to reflect back on the events of your life and find examples of both.

Times when fear spurred you on to triumph.

Times when fear dragged you down into defeat.

Have you got those in mind? Good. Then here's the crucial point: all of those battles, the triumphs, the defeats, *took place in your mind.*

You may have noticed something about the Afghanistan scenario I described above. We never actually used our guns. Nor threw any punches. We were Navy SEALs, as well trained in the art and science of shooting weapons and using physical force to fight as anyone on the planet. But none of that helped in this situation; there were no tools or technologies, no show of force or fighting skills involved. We did not have the higher ground. We did not have superior numbers. We were not on home turf. We had zero advantage.

The only weapon used here was a mastery of fear.

This book is not about facing down hostile gangs of men with guns in war zones. It's about the battleground in your mind. It's about your relationship with fear, and the dozens of situations—the thousands of situations—that you *will* face, and the fact that in those situations, fear can smother you, or it can liberate you.

It depends on what is happening between your ears.

Mastering fear is not about becoming physically stronger, or tougher, or more macho, or more aggressive, or more stoic, or more pumped up. It is about learning how to identify and change the conversation in your head.

KEEP THE SHARKS OUT OF YOUR HEAD

Let me ask you a question: What are you afraid of? I don't mean "concerned" or "a little nervous." I mean genuinely terrified. Are you afraid of flying or of heights? Of the dark? Close places? Drowning?

What about public speaking? That's a big one; people often rate it as worse than their fear of death, which is saying quite a mouthful.

Are you afraid that the right one will never come along, and you'll die lonely and alone? Or maybe you're afraid of commitment. I see that one all the time, and not only in relationships but in business and careers, too: people who are afraid to go all in, to push all their chips to the center of the table. Because what if you lose? What if the business doesn't work out, or the relationship goes sour, but once you're in, you're in, and you don't know how to get out?

I've known people who are intimidated by using the telephone, or a spreadsheet, or by the prospect of filling out a one-page form. Or swimming. A lot of people have fears that others might find ridiculous. It's not ridiculous, though, when it's you.

Are you afraid of failure, and the humiliation you're afraid will come with it? Or of success, and the crushing burden of responsibility you're afraid will come with that? Everyone's afraid of something.

For me, it was sharks.

"HEY, BRANDON, WAKE up, dude. Get your shit on. Anchor's stuck."

It's the middle of the night. I am already forgetting what dream it is I'm being so rudely shaken out of, but I know it was a lot more pleasant than whatever reality I am about to face. I am thirteen years old, a freshly certified scuba diver, working my first real job as an assistant on a dive boat off the coast of Southern California. Right now we are anchored off the backside of San Miguel Island, the northernmost of the Channel Islands, where the weather gets so rough it sometimes limits even commercial fishing boat traffic. Our fearless leader, Captain Mike, figures that if the weather gets rowdy, the boat starts rocking, and our paying passengers get too uncomfortable, we can always pull up and move to calmer waters.

Apparently, the weather's gotten rowdy. Time to move.

It's Captain Mike who's shaking me awake from that dead REM sleep. I open my eyes, but my brain is still asleep.

"Hey," he says again. "We need to move. The anchor's stuck."

Sometimes, when you go to pull up anchor, the damn thing gets caught up on something down on the ocean floor, a big ledge or chunk of reef. You can work your way out by patiently maneuvering the boat, but that can take an hour. It's much quicker and easier to send a diver down to find the problem and untangle it.

It takes me a moment, but I finally make the connection. He's saying that someone needs to go get our anchor unstuck—and that someone is me.

It's not only the weather that's different around San Miguel. The environment is different, too. It reminds me of this television show, *Land of the Lost*, about a family that goes back in time. You dive down thirty feet and it's like you're in a prehistoric aquarium. I've seen big abalones, lobsters, monster lingcod and rock cod, the kinds of fish you'd have to go down to three times this depth to find around the southern islands. On San Miguel's backside, where we now are, there's a massive sea lion habitat called Tyler Bight.

And one thing I know about sea lions: they attract great white sharks.

I have this thing about sharks. It's not just that they're dangerous. It's that the guys on the boat have been talking about them, telling me all sorts of stories about them. This area is a known breeding ground for sharks. Captain Mike, that crazy son of a bitch, has even raised a bunch of money to finance a shark hunt. Put together a few hundred pounds of fish blood and guts for bait and sat out there on the edge of the deck, trying to bait a great white so he could spear the goddamn thing. Like Moby-Dick is out there and he's Captain Ahab. By this point the whole thing has stoked my fear of sharks to a hot flame.

And now he wants me to go over the side? In the middle of the night? *No fucking way! There's no force on earth gonna make me go down there!*

That's what I'm thinking. What I say is "Okay." I *could* say no, but I don't want to lose my job, and I also really don't want to be "that kid who chickened out."

I scoop hot water from the hot tub into my wet suit to warm it up, then slide into it and head to the front. Most passengers go in off the back of the boat, but for the crew, the guys just swing open the bow gate and we jump off from there.

The guys open the hatch. I dive.

I plunge down pretty fast, clearing my ears, shining my dive light, doing my best to peer through the churned-up muck. I haven't done much night diving yet, but I already know visibility is not very good at night. With the sea swell from the weather churning up the floor, it's even worse than usual. If I encounter anything big down here, I probably won't see it until I'm right on top of it.

I try not to think about it.

At the edges of my peripheral vision, sea lions zip past. *That's good*, I tell myself. If there are sea lions here, that probably means there are no sharks around. Or maybe that just means me and my sea lion friends are all about to be so much chum in the water.

I try *hard* not to think about it.

I've done this maneuver once or twice in the daytime, just enough so that I know the routine. You dive down, trace the anchor chain, locate the problem, take your regulator out of your mouth, and blast a bunch of bubbles for a few seconds to give the crew up top a signal. They go slack on the anchor chain so you can maneuver it. Now you swim the chain around the reef and get to work getting the damn anchor unstuck. Once you do, you give the signal by blasting a second round of bubbles, and they start pulling. You stay with the chain until the anchor comes up off the bottom, at which point you give your third and final blast of bubbles, and up you go. So: I swim down and find the chain stuck under a massive ledge. I give a blast of bubbles, wait for the slack, and swim it around. It seems to take forever.

I make a massive effort *not* to think about sharks.

Finally, the anchor comes unstuck. I swim back up to the boat as fast as possible and haul myself out of the water in a rush of pride and relief. *Especially* relief. I get out of my wet suit, dry off, and crash back on my bunk, but I'm too wired to sleep.

At first I'm reexperiencing how good it felt to clamber back up on deck, and how lucky I was to get out of there alive. Gradually, though, those thoughts recede and a question slips in: Just how likely was it that a shark would have come butting in on my operation?

Honestly, how great *was* the danger?

At the time, I wondered how the hell Captain Mike and the other guys could be so thoughtless as to tell this thirteen-year-old kid shark stories that would scare the crap out of him, knowing damn well that sooner or later I'd have to go down there. Looking back now, I realize they weren't thoughtless at all. They were testing me.

Or to put it more accurately: they were giving me an opportunity to test *myself.*

It was the first time in my life that I came face-to-face with gut-wrenching, skin-crawling, testicle-shrinking fear. It was also the first time I understood that the actual physical situation in front of me was nowhere near as bad as the story I was spinning about it between my ears.

IT DIDN'T HAPPEN that night, but about a year later I did come face-to-face with my first shark, a big blue off the Southern California coast. Blue sharks are not particularly known for biting humans. Still, a shark is a shark. A blue will typically grow to anywhere from six to nine feet long. This guy, in other words, was a hell of a lot bigger than me. And he had teeth the size of jackknives. One bite from him could ruin my whole day.

I looked at the shark, the shark looked at me—and I felt it: that static charge. Years later, as a sonar guy in the navy, I studied how sound waves travel and propagate underwater. This was like that. An electric current running from his eyes to mine and back again.

I see this now all the time on the subways in New York. As I step into the car, I look left and right, sizing everyone up. When I lock eyes with a predator, some dude who's up to no good, or some street guy who's got something not right going on with him, he knows I see him—and that I am not letting him into my head. That guy is not going to mess with me.

This is not about trying to project an attitude of physical toughness or belligerence. It's purely about your interior monologue. When the conversation in your head is one of respect—I respect you, and you sure as hell need to respect me, because I am not looking for trouble and you are *not* getting into my head—then people pick up on that. If you send out nervousness, anxiety, and the signal that your fear is taking over, people pick up on that, too.

A vampire cannot enter your home unless you invite him in. So the legend goes. I don't know about vampires, but I know about sharks.

I've studied bouncers at New York bars and the security guards who watch the front door at Macy's. These guys are experts at reading people and putting a stop to trouble before it starts—and 98 percent of it is the conversation they're having in their heads. *I see you,* it says, *and there is going to be no trouble here. There are no targets here. These are not the droids you're looking for.* Yes, it really is some kind of Jedi mind shit.

Which is what I did that day in the water off the coast of California, staring eye to eye with that big blue. *You do* not *want this to go down,* my look said. *Neither do you,* said his. He moved on. So did I.

This is not purely about sharks, or sketchy characters on the subway. A shark can be any threat, or any *perceived* threat, which is not always the same thing.

When was the last time you felt anxious? What was it about? A deadline? An unpaid bill coming due? An important meeting ahead? A difficult conversation that you knew you had to have but were afraid to face? Think back to that moment of anxiety, that edgy, clammy-palmed feeling about whatever event or issue was swimming your way.

Next time that happens, here's what you tell yourself: "Whatever it is, you'll deal with it in its time and place. Meanwhile, don't let it swim around inside your head!"

I'll tell you a secret about the image on the cover of this book. You know, the warrior fighting the wild lion. Chances are good you saw that lion and figured it represents fear. It doesn't. The warrior on the horse—that's you. And that wild beast? That's your own negativity. Your sense of defeat.

The sharks you let in your head.

That's what we were battling in that ravine in Afghanistan. Not the Afghan guys with the guns. Our own interior monologue. If we'd thought, *Oh, we are so screwed, what do we do now?* it would not have ended well. But all three of us flipped the conversation in our heads to this: *There is going to be no trouble here.*

We did not invite the sharks into our heads.

A SNIPER'S SECRET WEAPON: THINK POSITIVE

After returning from Afghanistan, I began teaching advanced sniper programs for Naval Special Warfare. In late 2003 my SEAL teammate Eric Davis and I were tapped to help redesign the core SEAL sniper program, often considered the gold standard of sniper training worldwide. By then U.S. forces were already hip-deep in Iraq, and it was becoming clear that the so-called War on Terror was not going to be quick or easy. In this new form of warfare, Special Operations resources such as SEAL snipers would play a key role. We needed to completely rethink our approach to sniper training.

We revamped the course from top to bottom. We brought in new technologies. We moved our guys from hand-drawn sketches to advanced software and satellite communications. We upped their technical weapons training and turned them into ballistics experts. We trained them how to operate as solo performers and not exclusively in two-man shooter-spotter teams. But the single biggest advance we made, the one addition to the program that I am most proud of and that I believe made the biggest difference in the course, a difference that took our attrition rate from more than 30 percent down to less than 1 percent and began turning out perfect scores on the range for the first time in the course's history, was this: we taught our students how to change the conversation in their heads.

Here is a simple model we used. A kid steps up to bat. His coach, or his dad, yells out, "Remember, Bobby, don't strike out!"

So what happens? He strikes out, of course. What else is the poor kid going to do? The coach has made him so focused on swinging and missing, has so amplified his fear of striking out, that it's all he can see in his head. He's got a hamster in his head running on that hamster wheel full tilt boogie: *Strike out! Strike out! Strike out!* So that's what he does.

What should the coach have done? Focused on reminding Bobby about what he needed to do *right*. Stand, breathe, keep your eye on the ball, and judge it keenly. If it's outside the batter's box, let it pass. If it's over the plate, swing and connect. Bring bat and ball together. Make your team proud. All that good stuff.

Which is more or less exactly what we did with our sniper students. We taught them how to self-coach. We taught them how to flip that switch and change the conversation in their heads. Yes, an entire generation of SEAL snipers, among the deadliest warriors on the planet, were trained in the art and science of *self-talk*.

The same skill set applies in the field of business, too, just as effectively as in the field of war.

When my friend James Powell was serving in the Marine Corps, he had the ambition to join the CIA. He decided to try out, and pretty soon he was sitting in a waiting room with a bunch of other candidates, waiting for his interview, surrounded by Navy SEALs, Green Berets, and other Spec Ops guys, people with degrees from Harvard and Yale and Stanford—and suddenly James felt like a turd in a punch bowl.

What the hell was he doing there?

The woman at the front desk asked him if he was okay. "You look kind of nervous there."

"Honestly," he told her, "I don't know if my résumé stacks up with these other people's." He nodded around the room.

She looked at him and said, "Look, if you're in this room, then there's a reason you're in this room."

It was what he needed to hear. Her comment allowed him to flip a mental switch. A few minutes later he was inside, acing his entrance interview. He went on to a solid career there. Today he is one of our top writers at our veteran-run news site at Hurricane Media, our go-to guy on all things CIA. None of which would have happened if he hadn't instantly changed the conversation in his head.

Over the past few years I've been running a podcast called *The Power of Thought*. My guest list has included a World War II fighter pilot, a world-record-breaking astronaut, legendary musicians, million-dollar entrepreneurs and billion-dollar hedge fund managers, and of course, Navy SEALs and Green Berets and other Special Operations warriors. In every one of those conversations, I've noticed this core character trait: the ability to see and flip that mental switch. To me, that ability to self-monitor and change your interior dialogue is one of the most critical faculties that distinguishes a mature, adult human, someone capable of functioning fully in the world. It's what takes you from victim mentality to being proactive; from blaming others to taking ownership of your situation and taking positive steps to change it. It takes you from being at the mercy of circumstance to being the master of circumstance.

It is what allows you to master fear.

Don't get me wrong: I'm not talking about denial, or telling yourself that the danger isn't real. You may have heard that bit of psychobabble about how "FEAR stands for False Evidence Appearing Real." Sorry, but that's bullshit. Fear means *the awareness of danger*. The word comes from the Old English *fær:* "calamity, danger, peril, sudden attack." There's nothing false or imagined about a group of pissed-off mountain fighters pointing guns at you, or a shark swimming toward you, or a business collapsing into foreclosure. Or falling off a ladder while you're changing your storm windows and breaking your neck. Here's a popular meme that *is* true: Shit happens. The world is dangerous. Life is fragile. Each moment is precious, and you know why? Because it won't last.

Fear is no illusion. Fear is real. Convince yourself that it isn't, and you're already dead.

But here's what happens: Far too often, we focus on that awareness of danger, and by focusing on it we magnify it, cause it to expand until it starts filling the space in our heads. We start having the wrong conversation about it. We spin this story and then keep telling and retelling it, like that hamster running on its wheel, over and over. Rather than our mastering fear, fear masters us.

When that happens, here's what you need to do: (a) become aware of it, and (b) redirect it. Flip the switch in your head.

This is not some vague, new age pop psychology thing. This is how battles are fought and won. It is how billion-dollar deals go down and outstanding careers are made, how destinies are carved and lives are lived as richly and fully as they deserve to be lived.

MAKE FEAR YOUR ALLY

One thing this book will *not* teach you is how to "overcome fear." I don't believe in overcoming fear, because I don't see fear as my enemy. In fact, my experience is that if you see fear as the enemy, then you've already lost.

Fear is not something to fight. It's something to embrace.

You may have seen the quote "What would you do if you were not afraid?" It's become one of those memes that people accept as divine revelation, as if it were handed down from Mount Sinai on stone tablets. But I'll tell you what my two teammates and I would have done that day in Afghanistan if we were not afraid: we'd have been taken prisoner, or shot. Yes, I get what that meme author was driving at, and I get that there's a good point in there. For me, though, here is a much more powerful question:

"What would you do if you WERE afraid?"

How would you deal with that fear? Would you let it stop you or propel you forward? Fear can be a set of manacles, holding you prisoner. Or it can be a slingshot, catapulting you on to greatness. Read the biographies of great men and women, and you find that people who accomplish great things typically do so not by denying or beating back their fears but by embracing them. Not by seeing fear as the enemy but by making it their ally.

The goal is not to eliminate the fear. You don't want that fear to go away. You don't want to step into the ring, onto the stage, or out on the battlefield all loose and laid back. Professional singers, dancers, actors, and speakers will tell you that the nervousness they feel, that pinch of anxiety going into a performance, is more precious to them than gold, that they can't deliver to the level they're capable of without it. You want that adrenaline running, those palms sweating, that stomach folding in on itself. Records are not broken in practice; they're broken in the pressure cooker of the competition.

Fear is a lot like fire. When it's out of control, fire is destructive. Learn how to use it, and you can do practically anything. Harnessing fire is what made human civilization. Harnessing fear can change the course of your destiny.

José Torres was one of the greats of boxing, an Olympic silver medalist (lost the gold by a single point) and the first Latin American to win the World Light Heavyweight Championship. His secret weapon was something he learned from his trainer, the legendary Cus D'Amato. When they were working together, José discovered something about his trainer that shocked him: D'Amato was deathly afraid of flying. In fact, he'd never set foot on a plane.

"Are you kidding me?" said José. "How can you teach me how to conquer fear in the ring when you can't even take a normal plane flight?"

Cus shook his head. "You have to be smarter than that, José. Fear is something you *must have* if you want to be a champion."

"You *need* fear," as José later explained it, "for you to understand when the guy is going to throw a punch *before* he throws the punch, to anticipate what the guy is gonna do before he does it. All that is triggered by fear. Having that fear—not letting it get the best of you, but using it to help you—that is the quality of a champion. Fear is one of the best friends a champion has."

You can use José's strategy, too. The next time you experience true fear or anxiety about whatever shark is swimming your way—that big bill coming due, that important meeting, that difficult conversation—don't waste an instant of time or ounce of energy trying to stop or evade the fear. Instead, use it. Embrace it. Make it your ally.

Rather than telling yourself, "I am not worried, I am not worried" (which you know is total bullshit so you don't believe it anyway), ask yourself, "Okay: how can I use this static charge to sharpen myself?"

Take a deep breath, then another. Sit high up on your steed. The challenge is real, not false, but it is its own size and weight, no more, and you are up to the task. Be aware of the fear, and focus on the swing. On bringing ball and bat together. *You've got this.* Be the champion you are.

MAKE YOURSELF DROWN-PROOF

I didn't know it at the time, but my teen experiences with underwater wildlife were preparing me for situations I would encounter years later in Basic Underwater Demolition/SEAL (BUD/S) training. For example, the sequence right in First Phase called "drown-proofing."

They tie your hands together behind your back with a strap, then tie your legs together at the ankles with another strap. Then you go in the water. You float for a few minutes, then they tell you to start bobbing. You sink to the bottom, fifteen feet down, then push back up and take a breath, then back down, up and down, up and down. Fifteen feet is not an insignificant vertical distance.

You do this for five minutes. Not an insignificant length of time.

Then they blow the whistle, and you have to swim laps, a few hundred yards in all. Your feet and arms are still strapped tight, of course, so you can't swim normally. You have to figure out how to sort of dolphin yourself along.

You have a few days to practice all this before they test you. Some guys freak out right in the practice and don't even make it to the test. They just wig right out—and they're gone: instant fail. What they don't realize is that if you don't let your panic get hold of you, this exercise is actually a confidence builder. At first, the sense of not being able to use your hands and feet as you normally would feels horribly limiting, even claustrophobic. But if you relax and go with it, you quickly realize that you can actually swim just fine that way.

There's more. Next you have a fifty-meter underwater swim. No push off the wall: you just jump in feetfirst, do an underwater somersault, then swim the length of the pool, touch the wall, and swim back again, all without surfacing to breathe. Honestly, if you can hold your breath and stay calm, it's not that difficult, physically speaking. But that's a very big *if*.

As the class touches the far side and starts swimming back, usually a few black out and start floating to the surface like dead goldfish. Typically, the instructors will pass those guys. They got really close, and hey, at least they didn't quit.

Others reach a point where they think they can't go on anymore, and they surface voluntarily to take a big breath. That's a fail. The truth is, they could have made it, but as they grew more and more uncomfortable holding their breath and thinking they were reaching their limits, they squandered precious resources fighting back the panic.

A few guys don't even try. They just face the exercise, back down, pack their bags, and go home. They've already drowned, without even putting a toe in the pool.

This isn't just about water.

You can drown in fear anywhere.

For example, take that common phrase "drowning in debt." Really? Yes, you may be *swimming* in debt. But *drowning*? That, too, is largely in your head. This isn't a Charles Dickens novel and we aren't living in nineteenth-century England. There is no debtors' prison here. You can be deep in red ink, starting from less than nothing, owing a fortune, and still climb out. People do it all the time. I've done it. You don't really drown in debt; *you drown in the conversation you're having in your head about your debt,* which shapes your actions, and thus shapes your reality.

Say you have a handful of creditors you can't pay right now. If you think you're drowning, you panic and start trying to gulp air. Maybe you avoid those creditors, don't return their calls, evade their emails, and meanwhile start taking ridiculous risks to see if you can make back your losses as quickly as possible. All you're doing is thrashing in the water, sinking deeper, and using up vital oxygen in the process. Instead, stay calm, conserve oxygen. Contact them all, make a rational payback plan (you'd be amazed at the terms you can work out when you demonstrate a sincere intent to make the debt whole), cut expenses, take a Small Business Administration loan to consolidate the debts and expand your business, or take on extra work or an extra job just for now, do whatever you have to do to start chipping away at it, a stroke at a time—that's *swimming*.

Remember James Powell, sitting in that reception area, waiting for his job interview at the CIA? That's what he was doing there: drowning in insecurity. That's what Bobby's doing crouched at the plate, staring over his elbow at the pitcher: drowning in the humiliation and ignominy of *striking out* in his head.

I see people drowning in inexperience, drowning in obligation, drowning in unhappy relationships, drowning in jobs they hate. Thinking they've run out of oxygen, run out of time, run out of options. It's not true, but they see it as true, and so they go under. The truth is, they could swim just fine, even with their hands and feet tied, if they would just change the conversation in their heads. But they've given up.

What they need isn't more capital, more income, more

oxygen. What they need is a new understanding of where fear is pointing them—and a roadmap for how to get there.

Which brings us back to my friend Kamal.

FOLLOW THE SIGNPOST

The only reason Kamal and I ended up in that week of swim lessons together is that we share in common the same personal credo about fear.

I've described fear as a secret weapon, a champion's best friend; as a catapult or set of manacles; as the awareness of danger, a sense of the peril in your path. These are all workable descriptions. But here is the most useful core definition of fear I've come across:

Fear is a signpost, pointing the way to the prize.

Here's how Kamal puts it. "I have this rule," he says. "If something scares me, it means there's magic on the other side." That's why he was willing to meet me at the pool. He knew it would be worth it.

Years ago Kamal walked the legendary Camino de Santiago trail across Spain (a trek that formed the basis for his 2017 novel, *Rebirth*). The entire route was punctuated by yellow arrows that someone had painted carefully onto the scenery to guide the pilgrims forward in the right direction. They showed up everywhere: on the road, on the sidewalk, on a rock, on a mailbox.

He still sees those yellow arrows today, says Kamal, everywhere he goes. We all do. It's just that we misread them. We tend to see these yellow arrows as signs screaming, "Danger! Stop! Go back!"—when they are really pointing the way ahead, whispering, *"This way! This way!"*

There is a word for those yellow arrows: *fear.* Often what we interpret as danger is really the spark of adventure, the electric buzz of sensing what's over the horizon. A signal saying *This is where things get exciting.*

A signpost pointing the way to the prize.

I love taking people up in my RV-6A, the little side-by-side two-seater I keep just outside Manhattan. I take them past the Statue of Liberty, give them a tour of the Manhattan skyline, show them Central Park from 1,500 feet. I've flown more than a hundred people up over New York City, and I never get tired of it. I've noticed an interesting pattern.

While some of my passengers are nervous about flying in my little plane, and some are outright scared, there are some who do the whole flight with absolutely no fear at all. And here's the interesting part: typically, those passengers who are not even the slightest bit nervous are also not that excited about it afterward. To them, it was no big deal. But those people who were the most terrified about going up? They're also the ones who get the most out of the experience. It means more to them. They overcame a bigger hurdle to do it, and they appreciate it more.

It's because that prize is on the other side of fear.

"Which is all well and good," you might be thinking, "but how do I *get* there? The prize may be sitting over there, but I'm still over here! So what do I *do*?"

That's the question this book is here to answer.

I promised I would tell you exactly what I did with Kamal to go from a place of panic to running cannonballs a few days later. It's time to follow through on that promise.

A ROADMAP TO THE PRIZE

Imagine that your life is a story, a fantasy adventure complete with goblins and monsters, impassable forests and impossible tasks, and a fantastic reward in store at the end of the road a ring, a treasure, a magic bird, the keys to the kingdom. You are the princess, or the prince, and this is your journey. Those goblins and monsters and forests and mountains are everything that seems to stand in your way—every danger, every hazard, every obstacle. Everything that comes between you and your heart's desire.

Fear is pointing the way. But just how do you *get* there? Here's how.

There are five legs to the journey; I call them *Decision, Rehearsal, Letting Go, Jumping Off,* and *Knowing What Matters.* Call this your roadmap from fear to the prize.

In my experience, the path to mastering fear starts with a

moment of decision, a personal commitment to meet that fear and take action, large or small, in the face of that fear—even if you don't know what that action is or how you're possibly going to take it. The what and the how aren't important right now. You're in the realm of pure decision. *I'm going to do this thing.* (That's *Decision.*)

Once you've made the decision, it's a matter of doing whatever you have to in order to organize and prepare yourself. (*Rehearsal.*) Once you've sufficiently prepared, there comes a point when you have to let go of whatever crutch, limitation, or safety blanket you've been holding on to that keeps you from diving in (*Letting Go*)—and then, having let go of the lip of the pool, to take action (*Jumping Off*), that first step off your former home base that launches the journey.

Finally, there has to be something that makes going through that whole sequence worth it. Something important— that is, important *to you.* (*Knowing What Matters.*) Often you cannot go that last action step, make that jumping-off leap into the abyss of the unknown, without first having a moment of vivid clarity where you identify exactly what this *most important thing* is.

All my successful encounters with fear, and those of my friends whose stories I'll share in these pages, have followed this same general pattern of five crucial and distinct steps.

This is exactly what I did with Kamal during that week in the New York Athletic Club swimming pool.

1. DECISION

Mastering fear starts with a decision.

When I had that initial conversation with Kamal about helping him learn to swim, the first thing I did was ask him to commit to a week. I didn't say, "Why don't you come by some time, and we'll see what happens." I didn't say, "You want to give it a try?" I didn't say, "Hey, come on over when you have time, and we'll work on this." I told him he had to come every day, at the same time every day, for one week.

He said, "Okay."

No hesitation. No *maybe*. He said he would show up, and he did. Right on time, too.

Decision.

2. REHEARSAL

Once Kamal made the decision to hit the pool, the question was, what should we do there? What I for sure was *not* going to do was what everyone else had done when they'd tried to help him swim, which was to push him to "get out of his comfort zone."

In most cases this is terrible advice. Most times, when people step out of their comfort zone, they just freak out. Why? Because they're not prepared. My first goal was to get Kamal prepared.

You don't start with what you *can't* manage. You start with what you *can* manage and then build on that. All the technique that all those other teachers had tried to get him to do—the arms, the legs, the kicks, the strokes, even the floating—all of that wasn't the point. That was all peripheral. The point was water and breathing. That's what waterboarding is all about; that's what the fear of drowning is all about. Water and breathing.

So we started with water and breathing.

"Here's what we're going to do," I said. "I'll have you take a breath and hold it. Then you'll lower your head into the water, just for a moment, and while you're in the water, breathe out, like you're blowing bubbles. I'll show you first. You don't breathe in, just out. Then as soon as you've done that, you lift your head out of the water again. Then take a breath in . . . and repeat the process. Okay?"

I showed him. He watched closely, nodded. Got the plan. Okay.

Now it was his turn.

I talked him through it. "Okay, big breath in—now, head in the water and breathe out. . . ." He lowered his head into the water, some bubbles sprang to the surface, and a split second later so did Kamal's terrified face. "Good. Now breathe in again" (he'd already done that—he was gasping for breath the instant he surfaced) "and now, face back in the water and breathe out, slowly this time. . . ."

He did, and surfaced again. There were some mistakes, some panic, some coughing and sputtering, but he got it. We did that a few more times.

Then we moved on to something else. I showed him how to kick his feet, had him practice with a kickboard. There was nothing threatening about this whatsoever. The kicking itself wasn't even all that important, honestly. The idea here was just to get him comfortable with being in the water and having control over his body. The critical piece was already behind us: water and breathing.

Notice: he wasn't *swimming*. He was stretching his comfort zone.

Rehearsal.

3. LETTING GO

The second day we practiced the same things again: breathing in while above water, then dunking and breathing out; surface and inhale, dunk and exhale. And kicking.

By now he had gotten this down, but it was all still happening right at the edge of the pool. The moment he felt uncomfortable he would reach for the wall. I knew how to deal with that.

I said, "I want to give you a demonstration." I told him I was going to show him how a lungful of air would keep him afloat. I explained that when you stretch your body out on the water's surface and fill your lungs with air, they act as a buoyancy compensator, like the tanks you use when you scuba dive. "Watch."

I took a deep breath, and then, while holding it, I pushed

off . . . and floated. He just watched me. I just floated. Then I let my breath out, loudly (so he could hear it), and started to sink.

"Oh, my God," he said. "I get it. That really works."

"Your turn," I said. "Take a deep breath . . . and hold . . . and now push off."

He did. He stretched his body out and drifted away from the wall, just a very short distance, and floated on his back, just like I'd done. Then, when he couldn't hold his breath anymore and started letting it out, he began to sink—and grabbed for the wall.

"Okay," I said. "This is the next part. You have to stop reaching for the wall. So do this: when you start to feel uncomfortable, instead of reaching for the wall, just take another deep breath, and float on your back."

It took him a few tries, but eventually he got it. The first time he did, I could practically hear the *click!* He had a lifetime of training telling him to make a grab for that pool wall the moment he felt unsafe, but now he had supplanted that impulse with a new training, and instead of reaching for the wall, he would flip to his back and float.

Letting go.

4. JUMPING OFF

Remember that drown-proofing exercise from BUD/S, where they strap your hands and feet together and have you bob up and down in the water? Now that he was okay letting go of the wall, I did this with Kamal. I didn't tie his hands and feet, of course. And I did it with him, the two of us facing each other. Down we went, looking into each other's eyes, and up to the surface again. Like synchronized swimmers. Synchronized bobbers.

Again, this did not go perfectly. A few times he panicked and immediately surfaced. But still, he did it. "I can't believe I'm doing this," he said in between dunks. He said it more than once. Gradually, his fear began to relax. By the end of that session I had him on the bottom of the twelve-foot section, sitting there cross-legged, holding his breath, serene as could be. Then he would push up, go to the surface, take a breath, and go back down to sit.

On day three we practiced everything we'd done on days one and two, and then I showed him how to do a gentle sidestroke, kicking with his head out of the water the whole time. Then I showed him how to kick on his back, breathing slowly in and out as he went. On his back like that, I had him go clear across the pool, then back. Then down again, and back again, and on for ten full laps. The NYAC pool is fifty meters long; a full lap back and forth is a hundred meters.

Kamal did a thousand meters that day.

Jumping off.

"Look at what you're doing," I said. "Forget about that kitesurfing issue—if you fell off a boat right now and you weren't even *wearing* a life vest, you now have the basics to survive. You just roll onto your back and do what you're doing right now. You're *swimming*, man."

That was it. From then on: cannonball.

5. KNOWING WHAT MATTERS

The funny thing about all this was that for Kamal, swimming itself wasn't really all that important. It wasn't as if he intended to launch a career as a lifeguard or a combat swimmer, or had any compelling reason to *have* to be able to swim. Not being able to swim wasn't interfering with his life in any substantial way. Sure, it was a social inconvenience. He didn't like going to parties at his friend's house and not being able to join in the fun at the pool. Still, not such a big deal.

But Kamal hated the idea of fear holding him back. As he put it, "I don't like being afraid. It really bugged me that I couldn't swim." It wasn't the *swim* part of that sentence that bugged him, it was the *couldn't* part.

It was important to him to swim, because it's important to him to *live,* and to live fully.

He later told me that doing that first cannonball off the pool's edge was one of the best feelings he'd ever had in his life. It wasn't the cannonball itself. It was the freedom of it. That feeling made all the fear worth it. That was Kamal's prize, the magic on the other side, and he's carried it with him ever since.

The panic still comes back sometimes, he tells me. Sometimes when he's in a pool, he feels it starting to grip him, and when it does, he just flips onto his back and floats and smiles. His happy place. His freedom.

That's your roadmap—your path from the fear to the prize:

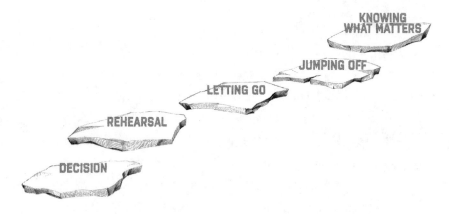

In the next five chapters of this book, I'll walk you through each of these five steps in more detail.

By the time we get to the conclusion, you'll be claiming your prize.

PRACTICE POINTS

Mastering fear is not about becoming stronger, tougher, or more stoic. It is about learning how to identify and change the conversation in your head. That ability to self-monitor and redirect your interior dialogue is what takes you from a victim mentality to a proactive mindset; from blaming others to taking ownership of your situation; from being at the mercy of circumstance to being the master of circumstance.

Control your interior monologue.

- Face the danger. Know that the actual physical situation is nowhere near as bad as the story you're spinning about it in your mind. Whatever the challenge is, tell yourself: You'll deal with it in its time and place. Don't ruminate. Don't let the wild beasts of negativity and defeat roam around in your thoughts. Don't invite the sharks into your head.

- Flip the switch. Focus on positive action steps you can take, not on the possible threats or risks involved; on what you aim to *do*, not on what you hope to *avoid*.

Make fear your ally.

- Think back to the most recent moment you experienced any kind of fear or anxiety. Close your eyes and put yourself back in that situation; bring it up as vividly as possible.

- The moment you feel the fear again, take a breath—and feel that electric charge of fear as the buzz of excitement, pointing you toward the prize.

- Now ask yourself, "How can I use this static charge to sharpen myself?"

- Memorize the steps above so that you can execute the sequence swiftly and firmly the next time you experience a fresh fear situation.

1

DECISION

Burn the boats.

—ALEXANDER THE GREAT,
upon reaching the shores of Persia, thereby cutting
off his army's only means of retreat

M Y FACE IS grinding into the sand, my body is beyond
exhausted. Four terrifying men are clustered around
me, screaming at me and doing their best to kill me.

Not physically kill me. I'll grant you that. They aren't going to ship me out of here in a body bag. But make no mistake:
They are planning to ship me out. Today. They want me as
gone as last week's breakfast, and they are here to make sure
that happens.

Basic Underwater Demolition/SEAL training is famous
for three things. First, that image you've probably seen, a line
of guys running on a beach, miserable but determined, carrying an insanely heavy log on their shoulders while being
yelled at by their instructor.

Second, the fact that there's this brutal ordeal somewhere in there called "Hell Week."

And finally: the quitting. The desolate row of empty class helmets lined up on the asphalt, marking the passage of the vanquished, the goners, the losers. And hanging over the helmets, that evil brass bell: the bell you step up to and ring three times to make your defeat official. The bell you ring to tell all your instructors and your teammates: "I give up. I quit." In BUD/S, the quitting never stops.

In fact, it starts even before the first day.

Lying here facedown on the beach, my teeth biting on sand, I have a clear recollection of the day I showed up for registration ten weeks ago, sitting on a bench by that concrete-and-asphalt grinder, watching a BUD/S instructor pushing another class of SEAL candidates through their punishing routine of PTs (physical training, i.e., calisthenics), and being scared nearly out of my mind. *Holy shit.* Seven months of *that*?

There are plenty of would-be SEAL candidates who reach this point and don't even make it through the check-in process. All it takes is witnessing another class being put through their paces, and their SEAL ambitions crumble to dust. I understand why. The truth is, I had a hard enough time just passing the quals to get *into* BUD/S, forget getting *through* it. I was coming off years of regular navy service, the fat fleet guy fresh from his cushy tour on the USS *Kitty Hawk* and checking into BUD/S after barely passing the SEAL entrance PTs. The guy the other candidates will look down on and the instructors will mark right away for early elimination. Of the 220 guys in my BUD/S class, I was the guy nobody wanted to be. *"That* guy." That was me.

At the other end of the spectrum was Lars, a supremely athletic guy at the top of our class. An incredible specimen. Lars had thighs like tree trunks and could do push-ups from dawn till dusk. He could do anything you threw at him. He wasn't human.

And in our first week of training, about four thirty in the morning, Lars quit.

We couldn't believe it. The guy we all looked up to, the guy we all would have pegged "most likely to succeed" was *gone,* nothing left to say he'd ever been there but another empty helmet. Lying there in the dark, sun not up yet, hearing that lonely brass bell clanging out through the silence of the freezing morning air, I could practically hear the thoughts emanating from the heads of all the guys around me, guys who up to that point had believed they were doing pretty well. *Shit!—if* Lars *can't do it, then* I *don't have a snowflake's chance in hell!* By the time we got through our initial indoc period and entered First Phase of actual training, 10 percent of our class quit.

And now, here I am, on the beach near the end of First Phase, and oh boy, only five months of torture to go.

If I survive this particular, personalized torture, that is.

For a lot of guys, the moment of reckoning will come in a few days, when Hell Week starts. Not me, though. For me,

Christmas has come early this year. This afternoon, these four professional sadists came over to our team and pulled me aside, separating me from the herd like a doomed wildebeest plucked by a pride of lions, and walked me out onto the beach, alone. Where they are now pushing me through an endless series of calisthenics, all the while shoveling sand in my face and screaming insults at me, all four at once, at the top of their lungs.

They've been doing this now for, oh, close to an hour, or maybe it's been close to a year, I'm really not sure at this point.

This is not a test, I tell myself. These guys are not trying to "see what I'm made of." They already know what I'm made of, I'm made of dirt and shit and weakness, and they don't like me, not even a little. They see me as a handicap to the team, and they are right. They want me gone, and if I were in their shoes, that's exactly what I'd want, too. They are *willing* me, with all the persistence and verbal abuse and sheer force of intention they can bring, to crawl from the beach up to the asphalt and ring that goddamn brass bell. I get it.

I look up at my instructor and tell him to go fuck himself. The only way they are getting me out of here will *be* in a body bag.

He drills me with a look that could bore a hole in a concrete slab. Then nods and lets me up. He looks over at his colleagues and says three words: "We're done here."

He can see it in my face: *I've decided.*

OF THE 220 guys who started out in my BUD/S class, fewer than two dozen made it to the end. That afternoon on the beach in First Phase, I realized two things. First, that I was one of that handful who would be going all the way through. And second, why it was that so many others wouldn't. And it wasn't about weakness, or because it was hard.

The reason so many guys quit was just this: they never really *started*.

Those of us who went all the way through BUD/S were not the strong ones. Not the ones with greater ability or an excess of toughness. We were just the ones who had *decided to do it*.

Mastering fear starts with a decision. You might think that big decisions, potentially life-altering decisions, arise out of courage. They don't. It's the other way around. The strength and the courage to keep going arise *out of* the decision.

The decision comes first.

DECIDE TO DECIDE

Decisions don't just happen. You have to make a conscious choice to be someone who makes decisions. You have to decide to decide.

I know that sounds circular, but it's the rock-solid truth.

Plenty of people go through their entire lives never really making decisions. Not big ones, anyway. Sure, they may decide what to watch on TV, or which socks to put on that morning. What to major in at college, which career path to go into. But even those larger life choices are, for far too many people, decisions they more or less slide into, not out of any soul-shaking reflection and commitment, but more because it's just what seems to come next. Maybe it's what their parents did, or what an older sibling did, or what the people around them expect them to do. What their friends are doing. What seemed like the most reasonable choice at the time.

For me, that's not a life lived, or at least not lived fully. And it's surely no way to master fear.

The first and most critical step in mastering fear is to make a decision that has its roots deep in your bones, deep in your character, deep in your soul. To do that, you have to choose to be the kind of person who *makes* decisions like that.

You have to decide to decide.

I learned this from my dad, and at the time, I hated it.

My family lived in the mountains of British Columbia until I was eight years old, when my dad decided it was time to pursue a dream he and my mom had to sail around the world. They bought a boat and sailed us down to Ventura, California, where we lived aboard that boat for the next seven or eight years.

Living on a sailboat in California was something like living in a trailer in Texas. At school, I was "the boat kid." As far as I was concerned, it was a great life; I would go surfing every morning before my classes started. I'd been working on that dive boat since the age of twelve, and I loved it. By age fifteen I was living a fantastic lifestyle, making good money, selling lobster I caught to my restaurant owner friends (probably illegally), and looking forward to turning sixteen, getting my driver's license, and chasing girls.

Then one night my dad made an announcement. "Everyone around here talks about the trip they're going to take someday," he said. "They're going to sail here, sail there, blah blah blah. I don't want to be the guy who talks about it his whole life and never does it."

Then he said, "We're going." And he meant it.

I was mightily pissed off. I loved my life just the way it was. I didn't want to go off on some family trip. But off we went. My parents enrolled my sister and me in independent studies, and next thing we knew we were sailing down the coast of Mexico, embarking on a thirty-day passage into the heart of the Pacific thousands of miles away.

By the time we reached the Marquesas Islands, my dad and I were arguing over some questions of correct seamanship. Eight hundred miles later, when we reached Tahiti, the friction between us had gotten so bad that it was clear one of us had to go. It was his boat, so the one who went was me. The next day I was standing on an island in the South Pacific saying, *Shit, this is for real.*

When the family boat set sail from Tahiti, I was no longer on it.

I left behind everything I'd brought with me, which was pretty much everything I owned: all my dive gear, a spear gun, a knife collection, a ton of books. All my worldly possessions. My parents helped me find a crew that was headed to Hawaii. (And by "crew" I mean a young couple with their three-year-old son on a forty-foot catamaran.) For the next two weeks my hosts and I made our way north, bound for Hilo on the open water. Here I was, just turned sixteen, my childhood home behind me and gone forever, alone on the Pacific. The first few nights, I cried myself to sleep. I was terrified.

When I eventually reached California, I had to face all the challenges of being a teenager on my own, learning how to do all those things I'd always taken for granted, even tasks as simple as shopping for myself, making dinner for myself, keeping my own laundry together. When I got that driver's license, I didn't even know how to put gas in the car. As scary as it had been to face the Pacific Ocean in a catamaran, in many ways this was even scarier.

And it was all because of those two words my dad had said. *We're going.*

My resentment burned like a blast furnace. Funny thing, though. Yes, I was furious at him, and yes, I was scared. At the same time, though, the strength and power of that two-word decision was undeniable. Looking back, I realize now that as angry as I was, I also drew strength from his example.

You've probably experienced this: a moment when you faced a tough decision, and then once you made it, everything suddenly felt clearer. It's like the first crack of thunder after a long buildup of low-pressure atmosphere. The air has been growing heavy and overcast all day, until that moment when the storm finally breaks—and then all at once the air changes. That's the clarity you get from making a big decision. And out of that clarity comes great strength.

Years later I learned about the great Irish explorer Ernest Shackleton, who was sometimes criticized by his contemporaries for being restless and eccentric. Others were impressed with his keen mind and unusual leadership style. Shackleton didn't care for authoritarian hierarchies; he liked to form a personal bond with each member of his crew. In selecting crew members, he cared less about people's technical qualifications and more about their character. And to Shackleton, character lay primarily in the capacity to be firmly resolute.

In 1914, Shackleton began preparing for one of the most ambitious trans-Antarctic expeditions ever mounted. To recruit suitable applicants for his new crew, as legend has it, he placed this ad in the newspaper:

Men wanted for hazardous journey. Low wages, bitter cold, long hours of complete darkness. Safe return doubtful. Honor and recognition in event of success.

Do you suppose the people who answered that ad were afraid? Of course they were. They weren't idiots. They knew that when he wrote "Safe return doubtful," he wasn't kidding. But their sense of adventure outweighed the fear. To a man, I have no doubt, they all read that ad and had the identical thought, the exact same two words my father spoke:

We're going.

LEARN TO TRUST YOUR GUT

So just how do you become someone who makes strong decisions? How do you develop that Shackleton gene?

It starts with *learning to trust your gut.*

This week I sat in a business meeting, watching someone who was faced with a critical decision. As I watched, he paused and looked up, like he was thinking about it—and I already knew he was going to make a poor choice. How? Because thinking about a decision doesn't make it happen. Thinking is just thinking. He knew this decision was coming. He needed to have already gone over all the options and considerations before this meeting started. The time for thinking was over. It was decision time—but he was still in his head. And decisions aren't made in the head. They're made in the gut.

Does that mean you'll always make the right decision? No. But I believe you'll get into far more trouble from *not* trusting your gut than you will from trusting it.

When I first got out of the service, I took my life savings and plowed it into a business idea called Wind Zero. It was a fantastic concept: a training facility serving both military and law enforcement personnel, deep in the Southern California desert. My research told me that the region was desperate for a reliable resource like this. Shooting ranges; tracks for combat and defensive driving instruction; mock urban environments for riot, hostage rescue, and other high-threat scenarios. Two helo pads and an airstrip. We even added a Grand Prix–style double racetrack, which reps from high-end race car clubs had told me would be in huge demand. Total cost, when the whole plan was in force, would come to something like $100 million.

Decision made. Off to the races (so to speak). I found the land, bought it, raised a few million in seed capital—my own savings plus investments from friends, former Spec Ops buddies, and family members.

It failed, catastrophically. Immediate cause of death on the coroner's report, if there were one, would have been "sustained pathogenic assault leading to system failure," the pathogen in this case being an extended nuisance lawsuit brought by the local Sierra Club. But like your typical terminal diagnosis, that doesn't tell the real story. What made us vulnerable to that external assault was an internal weakness. Our immune system was compromised. I had brought on a few key partners who were destroying the thing from the inside; that Sierra Club suit just came along like a high fever and finished the job. The real problem was my choice of business partners. I gave power and ownership to the wrong people—good people, no doubt, but a bad fit.

And the worst part of it was, I *knew* that. But I didn't listen to my gut.

It's called "gut" because you feel it deep down inside, and that means it speaks in a voice that's not always easy to hear. So how do you hear it? Same way you learn to do anything else. Through practice.

Some people seem natively better at this than others, people you'd probably call "more intuitive." But I wonder if they're really more intuitive, or if it's just that they have spent more time listening to their gut and less time being swayed by their thoughts. If you ask me, every one of us is natively intuitive. Some of us just haven't acted on it much. It's like a set of muscles that has lost tone through chronic disuse.

The only way to build your intuition is by exercising it, which means you're going to have to make some poor decisions. This is a good thing. You want to do that, because it's the only way to become effectively resolute, and not just plain stubborn. What's important about your poor decisions is that you follow through and act on them—otherwise you'll never see their true results—and then review them carefully, paying close attention to when you did or did not listen to your gut, and how that worked out.

There have been plenty of times since that business failure when I have failed to trust my gut, though thankfully none with fallout on so drastic a scale. I've had employees that my gut told me not to hire, but I let myself be overridden by others' opinions and hired them anyway, only to let them go later on after considerable trouble and damage. I've made investments that didn't pan out; formed other business partnerships that didn't work out; had relationships where I made poor choices. None of those situations were easy or fun—but they all helped me learn how to better hear that quiet voice inside.

One of my favorite executive directives comes from General George Patton: "A good plan violently executed now is better than a perfect plan executed next week." General Patton trusted his gut, and yes, it famously got him in trouble more than once. But it also won a lot of battles.

KEEP YOUR EGO IN CHECK

In sorting through the wreckage of the Wind Zero debacle, I realized something about my decision making. I had let myself be led by my ego.

This is shockingly easy to do. Because the truth about ego is, it's not a bad thing. A strong ego is healthy. Everyone who has ever accomplished anything great in this world, from George Washington to Steve Jobs, has been driven by an outsized ego—yes, even the saintly ones, the Schweitzers and Gandhis and Mother Teresas. (It's no contradiction to have a big ego *and* be humble.) The problem isn't having a big ego; the problem comes when you let that ego lead the way.

If you want to become accomplished at making powerful,

life-changing decisions, in addition to trusting your gut, you also need to stay *suspicious of your ego*. Because your ego is driven by feelings, and feelings are notoriously untrustworthy. There is a huge difference between having a gut intuitive sense about something, and having an emotional feeling about it. Part of the wisdom that comes with age and experience is the ability to recognize that distinction.

In 2012, after picking up the pieces from my failed first business, I started another, SOFREP.com, a blog site devoted to news and items of interest for the Special Operations community. Within a few years it had grown to become a multimillion-dollar media company called Hurricane, with a half dozen websites, a successful radio series, a publishing arm, and more. In 2014, I received an offer from a big media company that wanted to buy my business—for $15 million.

Getting that offer felt like a huge confirmation, a monster pat on the back, a "Hey, look how great you're doing!"—especially after the blow that Wind Zero failure had dealt to my confidence. I'd built this company up from nothing in only a few short years, and now some big player was willing to buy it from me for more money than I'd ever seen in my life. It felt amazing on a professional and career-move level. It also felt pretty damn good on the level of my wallet. This guy had just put on the table fifteen million very good reasons I should say yes.

But it just didn't feel right in my gut.

My ego said yes. My intuition said no. I turned it down.

A few years later that same company went through a hostile takeover by a group of Russian investors, there was a huge shake-up, and all the best people left. If I'd taken the offer and we'd become part of that company, it would have been a disaster. We didn't just dodge a bullet; we dodged a two-ton bomb. Chalk one up for trusting your gut.

Let me ask you: Faced with a tough decision, which should you listen to more, logic or emotion? It's a trick question: the correct answer is "Neither one." Emotional pull and rational argument can both be incredibly powerful—and they can both drown out the voice of intuition, if you aren't listening.

In any given situation where you have an important decision to make, practice separating the strands of logic and emotion. It's easy to get triggered by some aspect of the situation that evokes strong feelings, either positive or negative, and to mistake those feelings for gut intuition, then use logic to justify the choice you're already secretly wanting to make. This is a decision-making minefield.

This morning I talked with an investment banker I've been in discussion with who wants to work with my company and raise some capital for us. He checks a lot of boxes; there are plenty of green lights. But something just feels *off*. I don't know what it is, I can't put my finger on it, but something's not right. Even as I write these words, I can't tell you exactly what it is. But it's there.

I declined.

TAKE YOUR TIME

I know, it sounds counterintuitive. Not what you'd expect from a get-it-done type like a former Navy SEAL. But strong decision making is not the same thing as being headstrong. Rushing into a decision is not a sign of strength or confidence. Typically it's a sign of weakness. It takes strength of character to wait. Sometimes, a *lot* of strength of character.

Good decisions take wisdom, and wisdom does not reveal itself on a stopwatch.

It's important to be able to act, and act decisively. But there is a place for circumspection. Don't let yourself be rushed into making important decisions. It's easy to get so caught up in being busy that you don't take time to breathe, to think, to step back from the onrush of day-to-day details and focus on the big picture. The more plugged in to technology we are, the more important it becomes to take time, unplug, and slow down. Think of it as the care and feeding of your intuition.

After graduating from BUD/S, I joined a platoon at SEAL Team Three and spent the next eighteen months going through an extensive workup of additional training modules. At the very end of that process, as we were preparing to deploy to the Persian Gulf, we headed out to San Clemente Island, about eighty miles off the California coast, to pass a graded final training exercise (FTX), which our platoon had to pass in order to be certified to deploy.

We were getting some serious pressure from above to stay up late and work harder in preparing for this FTX. I was surprised and impressed at how our platoon chief, Dan Goulart, responded:

"No fucking way! We are *not* getting pressured into making bad decisions because of lack of sleep. My guys are going to get some shut-eye and be well rested for this mission. Because sleep is a weapon."

Sleep is a weapon. I've never forgotten that.

In the high-stakes world of business in a city like New York, sleeplessness and exhaustion are often worn with pride, almost as a badge of honor. I look at some of my friends who brag about working seven days a week, often around the clock. And yes, there's a time and a place for that kind of thing when you want to accomplish big goals against fierce deadlines—but you can't do it continuously. You can't make burning the candle at both ends your normal modus operandi, because it takes its toll and degrades your ability to think clearly. Which means you don't make good decisions.

When you go through Hell Week in BUD/S, you find out that you really *can* stay up for six days straight with no sleep if you have to. But if you *don't* have to, you're a hell of a lot better off.

When I look at my business colleagues, it startles me how many have not aged well. Some look ten years older than their age! I see this all the time, in media, investment banking, finance, any sphere of business: people juggling the hours and minutes like crazy, always angling to see, *How can I work harder, sleep less, cut corners, get that edge?* Ultimately they're doing the opposite of getting an edge; they're just killing themselves with stress.

One of my most prized secret weapons in business is that I take care of myself. I eat a healthy diet. I get a massage once a week. I meditate. Over the past few years, I've gone out of my way to take the time regularly to unplug from everything and give myself time to think. I have an insanely full calendar; still, sometimes I'll stop everything, right in the middle of the day, and just read for an hour. The clarity and perspective this provides helps me stay on top of my game. It helps me make better decisions.

If you want to make world-class decisions, you need to be fit, healthy, and rested. There's no way around it, no shortcut, no "hack."

STOP AND ASK FOR DIRECTIONS

Yes, it's a cliché, but like most clichés, there's more than a kernel of truth to it: men are famous for being unwilling to stop and ask for directions. Why? I have no idea. To me that seems like the height of arrogance. How is it a sign of weakness to seek out the voice of experience and consult people who know something you don't know?

Not stopping first to ask for directions almost got me killed once.

In early 2005 I was living in San Diego, working at the SEAL sniper program, and taking flying lessons toward getting my pilot's license. I'd just bought my first plane, a little Cessna 172, from a guy who lived out in Peoria, Illinois, when I had this brilliant idea: my best friend Glen Doherty and I should go out there, get it, and fly it back. Glen was also a SEAL and had just gotten his pilot's license, so that was perfect.

The two of us flew out to Illinois, picked up the plane, and got ready to fly it home. It was dark and rainy out, with a storm system on its way, but hey, we had instrument ratings. I figured we could get that puppy as far as Oklahoma that night, and make it the rest of the way the next day.

As we got up to leave the pilots' lounge and go climb into the plane for our trip, this old pilot shambled up to us and said, "You the boys just bought Bill's old Cessna?" We told him, yup, that was us. "You fellas really think it's a good idea to take this plane out tonight?"

That was all we needed. We looked at each other and both thought, *Dude, he's right. What were we thinking? It's February, it's storming out, and we're mortal.*

We got a hotel room and grabbed some sleep, then got up the next morning, filed a flight plan to Oklahoma, and took off in the light of day. That light didn't do us much good, though: once we got airborne it was too overcast to see a thing. Still, we figured that was no problem. We had instruments, and we had communications. At least, until we didn't. I was working the comms and soon realized that our radio wasn't working. We could hear the tower fine, but they weren't hearing us. Turned out, we couldn't transmit. Then we discovered that our glide slope indicator, which shows your angle on approach as you go to land, wasn't working, either. And our wings were icing over.

We looked at each other and laughed. "Hey," said Glen, "at least we have each other." It's good to keep your sense of humor when death is leering at you from just over the horizon.

We made a precision approach and managed to land at Tulsa using a handheld radio, a portable Garmin GPS, and no glide slope indicator. As tests of your stress capacity go, this might have been right up there with putting a drowning Seahawk helicopter down on the deck of a destroyer at night. Glen dropped that thing down on the runway, taxied to a stop, and we both took a breath. "Well, *that* was a little sporty," said Glen.

How would that scenario have played out differently if that old pilot hadn't put that simple question to us in the pilots' lounge? And if Glen and I had gone ahead and taken off the night before, rather than waiting for morning, what are the chances that things would have gone south, and I mean all the way south?

Making bold decisions does not mean throwing caution

to the winds. There is a razor-sharp line between bold and foolhardy. They may look similar. They are opposite. Being foolhardy is acting on all posture and bluff. That's not bold: that's just being stupid. The truly bold never throw caution to the winds; they steep themselves fully in the wisdom of caution, and then make the decision to move forward in the full awareness not only of all the dangers involved but also of their own capacities and limitations.

SURROUND YOURSELF WITH WISDOM

So how do you know when you're being bold and when you're just being stupid? The hard truth is, sometimes you don't. Which is why you need to surround yourself with people who know your business, or your project, or whatever it is you're planning to do, better than you do. This includes people who understand *life* better than you do, and yes, there are plenty of people who fit that category. In fact, just acknowledging that is a great step in a smart direction.

As I said, my first business ended in disaster, and not listening to my gut was one part of what took it over the cliff. Another big factor was my own inexperience. I've learned from both those mistakes. My second business has flourished. Since I turned down that $15 million offer it has continued to grow; today it's valued at ten times that number. And I credit the better part of that success to the fact that I've put a lot of energy and focus into building relationships with people who have more experience than I do, in all sorts of areas.

When they talk, I listen.

This is not always easy and not always comfortable. When I get together with my friend Nick Ganju, cofounder of Zocdoc, I know I have to watch what I say, because he will call bullshit on me immediately. Nick is smart as hell and totally unfiltered; he just calls it like he sees it, regardless of social niceties. If he's at a dinner party and he thinks the host is acting like a fool, he'll come right out and say so. Which makes some people shift in their chairs and look like they wish they were somewhere else—but for me, it's one of the reasons I love him. I have to be on my game, and I like that. If I'm going to engage in a conversation with Nick, it forces me to put my thoughts together. I can't go in half-cocked and bluff my way through it.

When I started Hurricane in 2012, I was living at Lake Tahoe, Nevada. Within a few years, I realized that if I wanted to build a media business I needed to be in New York City, so in early 2015 I picked up and moved. When I got here, I applied to join a business peer network called Entrepreneurs' Organization (EO), to put myself in an environment of learning and entrepreneurship. I met people like Solomon Choi, founder of 16 Handles, Ryan Zagata, founder of Brooklyn Bicycle Company, and Curtis Thornhill, founder of Apt Marketing. They have not only helped me up my game, they've also saved me from some dumb moves.

Joining EO was one of the best business decisions I've

ever made. The group puts on excellent events with amazing speakers, but to me its greatest value has come from being part of one of its forums: a group of seven or eight entrepreneurs who meet monthly to report in and update one another on what's going on in their careers. Peer coaching at its best.

My network started growing, and I made an effort to aim its growth at an upward angle, not a downward one, with people who had competencies I hadn't yet developed or who were performing at a higher level than I was. I knew that if you want to feed your ego, you surround yourself with people who look up to you—but if you want to feed your growth, you surround yourself with people whom *you* look up to.

Mastering fear starts with a decision. Which means that, if you are going to master your fear and thus become master of your life, you need to become a master decision maker. The single greatest strategy I know of for doing that is to *curate your environment.* Make conscious choices in what you read and what media you absorb—and especially in the people you spend time with.

Steep yourself in the ingredients of wisdom. In time, great decision making will become second nature.

PRACTICE POINTS

The path to mastering fear starts with a moment of decision—a personal commitment to take action, even if you don't know what that action is or how you're going to take it. Courage comes out of the decision, not the other way around. Make a conscious choice to be someone who makes strong decisions. Practice being decisive. Decide to decide.

Learn to trust your gut.

- Practice separating the strands of feelings and logic; listen to both, but don't rely on either one. Stay suspicious of ego. Trust your gut.

- Take your time. Don't let yourself be rushed into important decisions. Give yourself room to breathe and tap into your own wisdom. If necessary, take a step back and unplug. Think of it as the care and feeding of your decision-making capacity.

- Once you make a decision, follow through and act on it decisively. Don't second-guess yourself.

- After you take action on your decision, take time to sit down and examine how you made the decision and what happened as a result. What was your gut telling you? Did you follow it or not? How did that work out? Or were you swayed by emotional pull or rational argument? You can't avoid making poor decisions, but you can use them to hone your decision-making skills and deepen your ability to trust your gut in the future.

Curate your environment.

▪ Take an inventory of your environment, including what you read and what media you consume, including mass media and social media. Does it genuinely inform you? Does it challenge you, inspire you, stretch you?

▪ Take an inventory of the people you spend time with. Do they build your knowledge, your confidence, and your abilities? Do they stretch you? Are you surrounding yourself with excellence, knowledge, and wisdom?

▪ Seek out the perspectives of those with greater experience in every area where you are challenging yourself, as well as greater life experience in general. Cultivate a circle of colleagues, mentors, and advisers who challenge you to raise your game.

2

REHEARSAL

A lifetime of training for just ten seconds.
—Jesse Owens,
four-time Olympic gold medalist,
on the Olympics

One evening in April 2009 I found myself in a tiny studio room in San Diego staring into the eye of a TV camera. It was a few days after a team of three Navy SEAL snipers had rescued Captain Richard Phillips of the *Maersk Alabama*, and because I'd helped design the sniper course that these guys had gone through, CNN wanted to interview me on *AC-360*. Talk about fear of public speaking. It was the first time I'd ever been on live television, and I was about to talk to three million people.

When I look back at that 2009 footage now I have to laugh, seeing how stiff and uncomfortable I was. I did okay, but if you look close, you can see the terror in my eyes. Still, I had an advantage. I'd *trained*.

People who do this kind of thing all the time usually go through extensive media training to prepare them for live TV. I hadn't done any of that, but back in 2002, after coming home from Afghanistan, I had put myself through a four-week instructor training course offered by the navy. It was an illuminating experience. They didn't simply stand us up in front of the room to teach the rest of the group, they also videotaped us doing it, and we had to watch ourselves on replay, over and over again, dissecting all the good, the bad, and the ugly. Especially the ugly.

The fear of public speaking is a puzzle. What is it that we're so afraid of? It's not like the fear of flying or of heights. A plane crash or a fall from even a modest height can kill you. But getting up on a stage and talking to people . . . what's the worst that could happen? Just this: you could make yourself look like a total idiot, in front of other people.

We made ourselves look like total idiots, in front of other people.

Watching that first teaching footage was beyond embarrassing. It was brutal. We went "Um" and "Uh" and "Y'know" a thousand times, ten thousand times. We stumbled over words, spoke in nonsentences, scratched our balls, picked our noses, and looked like just about the stupidest human beings on earth.

Yet watching this footage over and over did not simply rub our noses in our own performances; it also got us gradually, slightly, marginally more comfortable with the idea of doing what we were doing. It was the public speaking equivalent of having Kamal put his face in the water and breathe out. It stretched and redefined the boundaries of our comfort zones. By the time I was on CNN live talking with Christiane Amanpour in front of three million people, was I nervous? Hell, yeah. But I was prepared. I'd gone through enough rehearsal that the fear didn't paralyze me.

Instead, it sharpened me.

That's the power of rehearsal.

You've probably heard this saying your whole life: "Practice makes perfect." Not true. Not even close. And this is important, because you need to know that once you sign the check, resign the position, buy the house, walk to the altar, or whatever the act is that commits you to a certain path, things will *not* go according to plan. If you believe that BS about practice making perfect, then you'll be taken completely by surprise when you launch into action and perfection is nowhere in sight.

Here's another saying, and this one *is* pretty accurate: "No battle plan survives first contact with the enemy." I also like Mike Tyson's version: "Everyone has a plan till they get punched in the mouth." There is no training that can prepare you for the reality of war, no rehearsal that can fully prepare you for the reality of starting your own business, no practice that will ever take away the ice-cold bath of fear that pours over you when you walk out onstage, step up to the microphone, or face the camera. Whatever it is you fear, make no mistake: when it comes time to actually jump off the cliff, you are jumping off a cliff, with all the terror that comes with it. No training can change that.

What it *can* change is what you do with the electric charge that moment of terror produces.

Practice does not create perfection. What it creates is *competence*. And that can make the critical difference. Competence breeds confidence. Not the swagger of false confidence; the quiet inner confidence born of knowing in your bones, *I got this.*

When our crew of four realized our chopper was plunging into the Indian Ocean, it wasn't our copilot's presence of mind alone that saved us. It was that, plus his competence. Both ingredients were crucial. The fact that he didn't freak out, that in that instant he mastered his fear instead of allowing it to master him, opened a fractional gap of space within which he could operate—and in that sliver of space his training kicked in. He could have had all the presence of mind in the world, the calm coolness of Bogart crossed with the equanimity of a Zen monk, but if he hadn't had those long months of rehearsal and preparation behind him, it wouldn't have done any of us a lick of good.

Practice does not make you impervious to fear; it gives you the tools to fall back on in that moment of maximum stress. Adequate rehearsal builds in a functional alternative to panic.

MASTER IT FIRST IN YOUR MIND

In the "Roadmap" I mentioned the mental management program my SEAL teammate Eric Davis and I brought to the Naval Special Warfare sniper program. Let me tell you about one of our main sources of inspiration, an Olympic shooter named Lanny Bassham.

Lanny was a child prodigy on the rifle. When he went to shoot in the 1972 Olympics in Munich at age twenty-five, he was already the youngest world champion in the sport and odds-on favorite to take the gold. At the last minute, he choked, and took the silver medal instead. That experience set him on a quest to understand the anatomy of reliable, consistent, gold-medal performance.

Two years later Lanny met a navy commander named Jack Fellowes who'd been shot down over Vietnam and spent more than six grueling years in a POW camp there, much of that time in a tiny cell where he could barely move. While incarcerated, he occupied his mind by improving his golf game in his head, visualizing every green, every stroke, every putt. When he was released and flown back to the United States, Fellowes got straight onto a golf course and shot par on all eighteen holes—better by far than he'd ever done before. His experience was not unique; there are quite a few documented cases of Vietnam POWs who poured their energies into mental rehearsal, and studies have found similarly astonishing results in subjects practicing basketball shots and other physical activities, purely in their minds.

Lanny spent the next two years interviewing nearly a hundred Olympic gold medalists and coaches, deconstructing everything they did and exactly how they did it. In 1976 he was back at the Olympics, and this time he took gold. He went on to dominate the field for years, winning twenty-two world individual and team titles and setting four world records. He also codified everything he'd learned into a system that he has since taught to coaches and athletes all over the world.

When Eric and I were redesigning the SEAL sniper course, Lanny came out to talk to us and share his approach. It was phenomenally effective. In fact, as I'm writing this chapter I just brought Lanny out to New York to spend a day with my team at Hurricane Media—because gold-medal performance is just as important in business as it is on the battlefield and on the Olympic field.

Effective rehearsal, Lanny taught us, starts in your mind. This is one of the prime secrets to mastering the fear of public speaking: see yourself on the stage, vividly enough that you hear the rustling of people shifting in their seats and feel your palms going clammy—picture it vividly enough that you feel the fear—and then use that fear to deliver the most electrifying presentation (in your mind, that is) that those people have ever heard. Relish the sense of mastery and presence, the sense of fulfillment and satisfaction at seeing your thoughts land in their minds and enrich their lives. Most of all, *walk yourself through the words,* making every point you want to make with precision.

That last is crucial: when you go through your mental rehearsal, focus on *doing it right.* I know, that sounds obvious. When it's "only" happening in your mind, though, it's easy to be sloppy and just kind of slide through it. Big mistake. Doing it in your mind doesn't mean that *how* you do it doesn't matter. It matters even more. If you're going over something in your mind in a casual, imprecise way, then you're training yourself to do it wrong. Mental rehearsal takes just as much discipline as physical, tangible rehearsal. Maybe even more.

And by the way, this approach isn't just a practice technique for shooting, or for when you have a speech to deliver, or any other specific skill to learn. This applies to how you frame and deliver your life. It applies to everything you do throughout your every waking day. To how you prepare and coach yourself to behave and perform in your business dealings, in your relationships, in your finances, in your health and fitness, in your friendships—in *everything.*

Because the fact is, you're *already* practicing mental rehearsal. Every day. Constantly. The only question is, exactly what are you rehearsing?

Here are three key steps you can use to master the practice of mental rehearsal, as applied to any and all areas of your life.

1. LISTEN. Pay attention to your thoughts. Start con-
sciously noticing your inner monologue and becoming
aware of what the voice in your head is saying. (Everyone
has one.) When you're alone, if possible, speak those
thoughts out loud, without filtering or editing them.
Whatever's going on in there, just vocalize it, let it spill.
You may be startled at what you hear.

If you notice your thoughts getting into a negative
spin cycle, going over and over that injustice, that person
who said something bad about you, that unfair boss, that
argument you had with your spouse/boyfriend/girlfriend
and what you *should* have said . . . *catch yourself*—and stop.
Because here's what is happening: You're rehearsing the
problem. Practicing how to make sure it goes wrong. Per-
fecting the damage. Just like Bobby at bat, drowning
himself in terror and humiliation as he tells himself,
"Don't strike out! Ye gods, whatever you do, don't strike
out!"—and in the process steeping himself in the dark arts
of the strikeout.

2. REFRAME. When you catch yourself in a negative spin,
take the time to sort through and figure out what you
would *like* to be thinking. Just like reframing Bobby's focus by giving him positive language—like "Keep your eye
on the ball, steady your breath, wait for a nice fat one to
come right over the plate"—reframe your own thoughts to

start mentally rehearsing what you *want* to have happen, not what you're afraid might happen or regret already happened.

3. FOCUS. It isn't enough simply to reframe from a negative orientation to a positive one. Once you've got your positive frame, you also have to sharpen that picture, hone those thoughts like a razor, so that they send a clear and unambiguous message.

When your thoughts are scattered, they don't have much impact, negative or positive. They are like diffused light. This is how most people wander through their day, going about whatever task is at hand as they shuffle their inner deck of random thoughts. Often these are predominantly negative thoughts, though there may be plenty of vaguely positive ones mixed in there, too. But there's nothing *intentional* there. Typically none of these jumbled thoughts are sharp enough to generate a clear image. How could they possibly yield a clear result?

Instead, focus your thoughts like a laser. Identify the specific sequence of events, actions, situations that you want to put into play in your life, then walk yourself through that sequence in your mind, as concretely and clearly as you can.

Rinse and repeat.

GET THE COCKPIT VIEW

When I take friends flying up over Manhattan, I want to make sure they have a good experience. As a pilot, I'm completely prepared—but I also want to make sure that as passengers, they're completely prepared, too. So the most important part of the experience happens before we ever leave the ground. We don't just buckle in and take off. First, I get my passenger in the seat next to me (the two seats in my RV-6A are side by side, not front and back) and show them everything.

"Look," I say, "I'm going to explain everything before we do it." I show them what goes into the preflight: how I check my various gauges and what they each do, how I go through my equipment, how I talk on the radio to the tower. After I finish that walk-through they'll always say, "Wow, I feel so comfortable now." They're not just being stuck in the back of the tube, where they'll make up all sorts of frightening scenarios in their heads. They're up in the cockpit, seeing exactly what's going on. Basically, I'm giving them their first flight lesson.

I call this *getting the cockpit view*.

In the SEALs I learned that there were two types of corpsman, or medic. One type would explain exactly what was happening, what he was about to do, and why. My best friend Glen was like that. The other type would just jam the needle in and tell you to shut up and hold still. Strictly speaking, they both got the job done. But the experience was different.

In redesigning our sniper course, Eric and I followed that show-them-first philosophy. As part of our course overhaul, we implemented a classroom module that gave our students a comprehensive understanding of the science of ballistics—the physics of how a projectile moves through space—prior to getting them out onto the range. Before they pulled their first trigger, they understood exactly what was going to happen when they did.

Cockpit view.

This is exactly what I did with Kamal in our first swimming lesson. I started by walking him through the whole process of submerging his head and then breathing out—before we did it. I explained how his lungs acted as a buoyancy compensator, demonstrating it myself, so he would understand the physics of what we were about to do *before* we started doing it.

People say "Familiarity breeds contempt," but in my experience that's exactly backward. It's complete *lack* of familiarity that breeds contempt, suspicion—and fear. But I'll tell you what familiarity *does* breed: competence and confidence. Which is why familiarity is the warrior's secret sauce, the antidote to fear.

Whenever you take on anything new, especially anything scary or intimidating, it's essential to first get that big picture, so you can see clearly what's about to happen, and that it's probably quite different from—and not nearly as frightening as—whatever you're expecting.

FIRST, *STAY* IN YOUR COMFORT ZONE

It has always struck me that when people say that in order to achieve great things you have to "get out of your comfort zone," this is basic bullshit. It's like saying, "Just *do* it." Well, great, but what if you *can't* "just do it"? I can picture how effective *that* sniper training program would be: "Here's a rifle, there's the target way over there, okay? Now, *just do it.*"

The problem with "get out of your comfort zone" is that it's a tactic that doesn't address the nature of the problem. It's a nonsolution, like saying, "Oh, you're afraid to jump? Well, just stop being afraid." Not helpful.

The problem is that going outside your comfort zone goes against your nature. There's a reason that comfort zone is there: self-protection and self-preservation. People talk about your "comfort zone" as if it were a bad thing, a measure of weakness or laziness. That's just stupid. Every phenomenon in nature is designed with a multiplicity of comfort zones. Your body works best at about 98.6 degrees Fahrenheit. Your optimum functioning occurs when you get roughly eight hours of sleep. It's probably a good idea to use that milk in your fridge *before* its expiration date. (Does anyone think waiting an extra month and *then* drinking that milk is a good idea because you're pushing it "outside its comfort zone"?)

It might help to redefine the concept with a different term: *competence zone.*

The key to effective rehearsal is to identify the boundaries and definitions of your current zone of competence, then apply *repetition* and *refinement* to deepen, strengthen, and extend those boundaries and definitions.

Here's an example. Say you're a pianist or guitar player and you need to learn a difficult passage that goes superfast. There's a right way and a wrong way to practice it. You can play it over and over as fast as possible, screwing up the notes right and left, and hope that through repetition you'll start getting more of it right. Or you can start out playing it slowly, with every note correct, and gradually pick up your tempo over time.

Guess which one works.

Playing the passage slowly is within your current zone of competence. So that's where you start. Playing the thing like lightning but fucking it up royally as you go will only train you to fuck it up royally. And leave you frustrated in the process. Because you're diving way outside your zone of competence.

The same thing applies to assembling a rifle. You learn the steps perfectly at a speed you can follow. Once you have them down, then—and *only* then—you start ramping up the speed.

And it's not just about speed. Sometimes it's about *scale*. Telling your story or giving your talk to a few friends, one at a time, is a great way to work out the kinks before taking the stage. Same with putting an idea into a blog post before submitting it to a publisher.

My friend Matt Meeker had this idea for a monthly box of treats and toys for dogs. Never meant it to be more than a little side project. A friend worked it up as a mock website and put it on Matt's phone, and Matt showed it to a few friends. Within a few months nearly fifty people had signed on to the idea. The product didn't exist yet, and neither did the company, but Matt had rehearsed the idea on an intimate scale— and it worked. Today Bark & Co. is a $100 million–plus business that has shipped more than ten million BarkBoxes.

Get it right on a small scale, and you've got a much better chance of taking it big—just like getting it right at a slow tempo is what it takes to play it fast.

There's a critical aspect to that speaker training course I took in 2002 that I didn't mention yet. That first talk we did, the one that we then dissected on videotape? It was only five minutes long. The point of the course was to prepare us to teach complete classes, which might last forty-five minutes or an hour, or even longer. Yet they started us each with a five-minute talk. Why so short?

Comfort zone.

I have a friend, Neil Amonson, who served as an air force combat controller. When my SEAL platoon was in Afghanistan, we worked side by side with Combat Control Teams (CCTs) and I admired the hell out of them. You know the old line about Ginger Rogers, that she could do everything Fred Astaire did, only backward and in high heels? CCTs are like that. (Minus the heels.) They go into combat with SEALs and Green Berets, ready and able to go anywhere and do just about anything. In many ways, these guys are the unsung heroes of the Special Operations community.

During the course of Neil's two years of CCT training, just like any SEAL candidate in BUD/S, he had to go through scuba school, land navigation/survival, and HALO (high altitude/low opening) jump school—and when he hit that last, his life changed. Neil fell in love. I don't mean with another person. He fell in love with flying through the air. He quit all his other hobbies and threw himself into skydiving. He's been a full-time skydiver ever since.

In fact, he loves anything that has to do with being up in the air—skydiving, paragliding, piloting a plane, you name it. He even spent a decade of his life BASE jumping—the most extreme, dangerous, terrifying of extreme sports. After three of the sport's top flyers died in a single accident in 2014, Neil hung up his BASE jumping hat, but he continues to spend as much time in the air as possible. "If I go two weeks without being up in the air," he says, "I start getting a little antsy. I always think something else is bothering me, that there's some other issue going on in my life—and then I'll suddenly realize, 'Oh, right! I just need to be back in the air again.'"

You might be thinking, "Okay, but why are you telling me this?" Because here's the part I didn't tell you yet:

Neil Amonson is afraid of heights.

I shit you not. The guy who joined the air force to become a combat controller, who fell in love with skydiving, who spent a decade as a BASE jumper, and who to this day is happiest when flying through the air, is afraid of heights. Not *was. Is.*

So how the *hell* did he get through HALO—and what made him go into the air force in the first place, let alone devote his life to skydiving and flying?

Neil answers with a single word: "Training."

It was that incredibly thorough, systematic, step-by-step training that nobody does better than the military. When Neil and his classmates went through HALO school, they started out by spending a solid week working in a wind tunnel in North Carolina. Hour after hour, for days on end, Neil practiced skydiving just a few feet off the floor in that indoor wind tunnel until he knew, from a physiological standpoint, exactly what skydiving felt like in every part of his body. (Cockpit view, big-time.) By the time he left the wind tunnel he knew down to the level of muscle memory exactly how to control his body in freefall. The only thing he hadn't done yet was jump out of a plane to do the same thing in the open air.

"This is something I really like about the military," says Neil. "For the most part, they have that crawl-walk-run way of teaching things."

The crawling part was the week in the wind tunnel. The walking part was going through the same moves after stepping out of an airplane. And the running? Doing the same thing with full combat equipment, in night jumps at high altitudes while wearing an oxygen mask, with other people, all at a fast pace.

Crawl, walk, run.

Neil never went on roller coasters as a kid, because he knew it would feel totally out of his control. But training to be a pilot didn't freak him out at all. He knew they were going to train him to be in control of this thing. After all, you can't spell "combat controller" without the word "control."

Which is another great term for "comfort zone"—it's not only your zone of competence, it's also your *zone of control*.

That's what Kamal experienced in those first few lessons in the NYAC pool: he never felt things were getting out of control.

THEN STRETCH IT

Of course, you'll never get anywhere by simply sitting there in your comfort zone. The key to a successful practice strategy is to take yourself from crawl, to walk, to run—*without* any sacrifice of accuracy along the way.

Back to that example of the musician practicing the difficult passage. As I said, first you practice it slowly, getting every note right, until you have it down pat. But then you have to speed it up—gradually at first, then pushing yourself to the point where you're playing the thing as fast as you possibly can . . . and then a little faster.

You soon notice you're dropping a few notes, messing up the passage here and there. No problem; slow it down again. Get every note right. Accuracy is paramount. Then accelerate once more. Push to the limits of what you can do—and then push a little further.

You're not forcing yourself *outside* the parameters of your competence—you're *magnifying* those parameters. Not stepping out of your comfort zone, but stretching it, enlarging its boundaries.

I learned this in BUD/S, going through a process we cheerfully referred to as *torture*. It wasn't, of course. That was just the term we would throw around to describe what our instructors put us through. In reality, what they were doing was the opposite of torture. The point of actual torture is to take you completely and emphatically outside your comfort zone, with no hope of getting back in unless and until you comply with the torturer's demands. The point of Spec Ops training is to stretch that zone so that you can tolerate your circumstances with equanimity even under the most extreme conditions.

Torture aims to break you. Training aims to build you so that nothing can break you.

It probably sounds strange to talk about BUD/S in the context of your "comfort zone." If there is any experience in the world that is as *un*comfortable as it is humanly possible to be, BUD/S would have to be it. But look at what they're really doing. When you see those guys running along the sand with that massive log on their shoulders, what you're watching is a group of people who are experiencing a profound shift in their definition of normal. This takes skill, knowing how to train to the limits but not beyond. Part of what makes SEAL training so effective is that the instructors have a finely tuned ability to observe and assess. They are watching every moment to see when stretch is about to turn into snap. Their goal is not for you to damage yourself, but to take yourself right up to the edge of damage.

This is one of the keys to effective practice: getting a feel for how far to push yourself. Beyond that push point it becomes counterproductive. Short of that point, you're not stretching.

My friend Curtis Thornhill, founder of Apt Marketing, is a genius at digital marketing. He also happens to be a committed adventurer with a lifelong passion for travel and the outdoors. When a friend called in 2007 and said, "Hey, I'm going on a tour of Africa, you want to climb Kilimanjaro?" he replied, "Sure." Two weeks later, the two were on a plane to Africa.

Curtis's friend chose one of the most difficult routes up, so it took them five days. As they neared the summit, the oxygen thinned and thinned and the weather got colder and colder. Curtis hadn't slept much, and by the fourth day he'd run out of water purification tablets, so along with his mounting exhaustion, he was starting to get dehydrated. In the middle of the night on day four, he reached his limits. He could not go even one step farther.

Just take one more step, he told himself. *That's all. Just one.*

He took a single step. Just one.

Then he went through the same process all over again: knew he couldn't go any farther, but told himself the same thing anyway: *Just one more step.* And took another step.

Then one more.

There's a popular saying on Kilimanjaro: *"Pole, pole"* (pronounced *polay, polay*), which is Swahili for "slowly, slowly." He was going *slowly, slowly,* all right, each step half the normal length, barely moving at all. Suddenly Curtis began violently throwing up, until it seemed as if he were turning inside out. Now he felt even worse. He didn't see how he could possibly manage even one of those feeble half steps.

A few long minutes went by.

Finally he thought, perhaps he could push a little farther, just one more half step.

Polay, polay.

They eventually managed to summit, and Curtis had his first mountaineering victory under his belt, an experience that left him with a sense of what it means to keep moving when you have no other option, and of how powerful the mind can be in the face of seemingly impossible limits.

Crawl, walk, run—and do the impossible.

PREPARE MORE THAN YOU NEED

The next time you watch a great movie, think about this: for every minute of screen time you're seeing, the director shot at least twenty minutes he or she never used. That's more than forty hours—nearly two whole continuous days—of footage, at the cost of millions of dollars, that no one will ever see. What a waste, you say? Not at all. It's standard operating procedure. That's what it takes to produce a great movie.

Great performance in *any* domain is like that. You prepare a lot more than you need. A *lot* more. In the course of one season an oak tree will drop thousands of acorns. Why? All it takes to safely reproduce itself and continue the oak species is a single acorn. So what are all those others? Rough drafts.

Great rehearsal is like that. You don't prepare for what will happen. You prepare for the hundred things that *could* happen but probably never will. You don't practice what you *expect* to do. You practice for that and ten times more, fifty times more.

In the spring of 2016 I flew to Fort Lauderdale to meet up with my old flight instructor, John Carey. I'd just bought a little plane, a single-engine Fuji LM2, off an old marine aviator. It was built by the Japanese in the fifties as an aerobatic military trainer, based on the Beechcraft T-34, the original single-engine, two-seat version. Which means this thing was serving in the Japanese defense forces a decade and a half before I was born. John had agreed to join me on its maiden voyage, taking it down to Miami and from there to Puerto Rico, where I'd be hangaring it.

I've known John for more than a decade, ever since my days in the military when I was getting my pilot's license and he was my flight instructor. John is a classic old-school aviation mentor, weathered face, scratchy voice that sounds like it has barked a million crew directives through a hundred thousand storms.

John and I went out to the airport to meet the guy who was walking us through our "new" plane before we did a test run. It was all pretty straightforward, but every plane has its little idiosyncrasies. When he started up the engine run, something didn't sound quite right to me, but the engine was making power just fine and everything checked out. So off we went, flying our short pattern.

The initial departure is always the most critical phase of the flight. You're low, which means you don't have a lot of altitude to glide the plane, which also means you don't have the kind of time to make decisions as you do when you're up high. You're also at the heaviest you're going to be, because you just took on fuel. And you don't have a lot of airspeed yet. Add that all up: you're heavy, low, and slow. That's why so many serious accidents happen in the seconds and minutes immediately after takeoff.

We started down the runway. Something still didn't sound right to me—but again, everything looked okay. Then we were off the runway and in the air. I was on the stick, John in the seat behind me, and I was expecting to hear his cranky voice shouting instructions in my ear, like the old days when he was first teaching me how to fly. Right now, though, John wasn't yelling anything. He was sniffing the air.

I smelled it, too. I looked down. My pant leg was soaking wet. There was fuel squirting out all over me.

Oh, shit.

There's a fuel hose that runs from the engine to the pressure gauge in the control panel. The end that connects to the panel had come off, and our engine's precious fuel pressure was now bleeding out all over my leg. Which meant I was sitting in a puddle of highly flammable plane fuel, in a plane that was almost as old as John. I glanced at my radios. All it would take was one of those suckers deciding to spark at that moment, and John and I would be sitting in a cockpit fire.

This was one of those situations where you want to be more prepared than you ever thought you'd need to be.

A major part of a pilot's training is the mastery of contingency plans. Pilots run dozens, hundreds of what-if scenarios. What to do if an engine goes out; if you spring a fuel leak; if there's an electrical problem; if you lose comms. When

Chesley Sullenberger glided that Airbus A320 to a safe landing in the Hudson in January 2009 with all 155 aboard safe and sound, they called it "the miracle on the Hudson." But the real miracle had already taken place years beforehand. Sully had *rehearsed* it. Nobody expected he'd ever need to actually *do* it.

Good thing he was overprepared.

The same is true for SEAL training, and all Spec Ops training. If your team is going to do a beach landing, or an insertion by helo in enemy territory, or a nighttime takedown in a village compound, there are a thousand things that could go wrong. When they do, we're ready for them.

For example, Operation Neptune Spear, the May 2011 raid on Osama bin Laden's compound in Abbottabad, Pakistan. When one of the team's stealth Black Hawk helicopters crashed, it could easily have spelled complete failure for the raid, death or capture for the two dozen SEALs involved, and total catastrophe for the U.S. military. But the SEALs had contingencies drilled into their bone marrow. They blew up the chopper, carried out the mission, and got their asses out of there, flawlessly, almost as if they'd *planned* to lose a chopper. Which they *had,* more or less, because whatever could go wrong, they'd rehearsed it.

In practice, they'd timed the mission at forty minutes flat. In actual operation, they were in and out in thirty-eight. That's some first-rate training. For Navy SEALs? SOP.

We have such an exceptionally strong standard of contingency planning for pilots and Special Operators because these are both professions that involve a high level of danger. We ought to have equally high training standards for civilian driver's licenses, but we don't. You think that might have anything to do with our horrifically high traffic fatality rates? Come to think of it, it might not be a bad idea if we implemented that kind of thorough contingency training for future parents, too, before they have kids.

You definitely want that same level of contingency planning in business. That's the purpose of a good business plan: not to show someone else so you can get financial backing, but to show *yourself* so you're prepared. A business plan is not just a set of numbers, it is a rehearsal. A walk-through. A smart business plan plays out multiple scenarios: not only the way you intend things to happen, but the various ways they might go down differently from what you expect.

The same thing is true for public speaking. When I say "know your material," I don't mean "have your speech memorized." I mean know your *area,* and think through what you really want to say. When being interviewed on camera, talking to a few million people, you don't get to deliver a memorized speech. And you don't have twenty minutes to find your way to your main points; you might have twenty *seconds*. You have to respond to whatever questions they throw at you—and chances are excellent that they won't ask the questions you want them to. You have to have your sound bites down, so you can come back with something that isn't evasive but that says what *you* wanted to say.

Contingency planning.

Whether you're an entrepreneur pitching your idea to a potential investor, or a salesperson making a presentation, or a teacher giving a class, or you're being interviewed on live television, you can never control or fully anticipate what the other person is going to say. All you can do is do your best prep, and then climb into the hot seat. I'll tell you what, though: that seat is a lot less hot when you know your material down cold.

Speaking of hot seats, you're probably wondering what happened up there in the cockpit of my Fuji LM2.

In a small plane like this, all the essential controls are mechanical, which means I should be able to fly the damn thing even with the power shut off. So before our radios or anything else had the chance to spark, I immediately shut down all our electrical systems. We made an expeditious landing and taxied back to our starting point, replaced the hose, and then took off again, bound for Miami and points southeast.

The only reason that little test flight did not turn into a disaster was that I didn't give it time to. I had that electrical system shut down in seconds flat. I didn't have to think about it.

I'd rehearsed it.

RAISE YOUR PREP STANDARDS

All of the foregoing really boils down to this: if you want to raise the level of your performance, in any area, then focus on raising the level of your *rehearsal*. Whether this is something you're already doing that you want to do better, or something that you've never done before and want to master, the strategic place to put your energy is in your own self-preparation.

Which means: Challenge yourself. Don't content yourself with resting on your laurels. Make it a singular effort, then a regular practice, and then a habit to assess where you are right now and stretch yourself 5 percent further.

Take your health, for instance; specifically, your diet. How accurately do your food choices build and support the level of health you aspire to have? I don't have one particular dietary approach or perspective I adhere to or endorse; I am just on the constant lookout for new information and powerful ways to up the level of my health through everyday food choices. That means reading about health and nutrition, hanging out with people who have taken a highly proactive approach to their diet and health, and always being open to new knowledge, information, and insights on the subject. And always challenging myself to be like the Olympic motto: *citius, altius, fortius*—faster, higher, stronger.

Here is the relevant question for this chapter: What level

of standard do you want to hold for yourself in your own practice? Whatever it is, I recommend you raise it, even if only by a marginal amount. That's what "stretch your zone of competence" means. If you already have an expectation of exellence, that's great. Now raise that 5 percent. And tomorrow, another 5 percent.

I have a friend who was participating in a series of entrepreneur networking events, which sounds like a good thing, except that he was already performing at a level beyond everyone else in the group. Which meant he was a big fish in a small pond getting his ego stroked by these wantrepreneurs who were all impressed with his accomplishments.

"Man," I said, "you're wasting your time. You need to be sitting down with the CEO of some software company who has just crushed it—the guy you're trying to become. A guy who can help raise you up, give you solid connections, and call bullshit on you when you need it."

I offered to connect him with some of my successful entrepreneur friends, like Solomon Choi (16 Handles) or Ryan Zagata (Brooklyn Bicycle Company), but he was reluctant to meet them. I understand why. When you spend time with someone who's powerfully successful in business, uh-oh: the stakes are higher. That's exactly why I *like* spending time with those people. I don't want to hang around with people who pat me on the back and tell me how great I'm doing. I want to be stretched.

EO had a really high revenue threshold to become a member, and when I joined that group in 2015, I was stretching myself. But I didn't stay there forever; in 2017 I left EO to join another group, YPO (Young Presidents' Organization), that has an even higher entry bar. YPO's membership roll includes the presidents of billion-dollar companies. That's what I'm shooting for now. It's been an exciting ride, to build my business from zero to the point where it's valued at $100 million. But I want to scale up. I want to build a business valued at $1 billion. To do that, I need to stretch my comfort zone, to access people on a business level that's intimidating for me.

I need to raise my standard.

When I started Hurricane in 2012, it was just a blog. It didn't take long to see that what I really had going was a full-fledged media business. I'd gone into it not really knowing all that much about media or advertising—but I made it my business to learn, and fast. I read, and read, and read some more, as many as a dozen books a week. It's now six years later and I'm still doing it. The clerks at my local bookstore know what I like, and every time I go in they have a stack waiting for me. I've read just about every book there is on media, advertising, and marketing from the past half century, or at least the titles that matter. And hundreds more titles on every topic that might be connected, even if only tangentially.

The average businessperson will get a handle on some area of knowledge by reading maybe three or four books on the topic, or even half a dozen. My approach is a little different: I'll read a hundred. Every time I bump into another topic

I need to know about, whether it's documentary filmmaking or investment banking or cryptocurrency, I go chow down on at least a shelf or two of books on the subject. Every super-successful businessperson I know does likewise, consuming a ton of great knowledge-based content on whatever they feel they need to know.

There's a phrase I've heard a lot of business wannabes and middle-of-the-road entrepreneurs use: "massive action." I guess it means something like, "If you throw enough pasta at the wall, something's bound to stick." Maybe that works for them . . . maybe.

For me? I prefer *targeted* action—coming on the heels of massive *preparation*.

PRACTICE POINTS

Effective rehearsal does not eliminate fear or make you impervious to fear; it gives you the tools to fall back on in that moment of maximum stress. Practice creates competence, which breeds confidence. It's a lot easier to be in the hot seat when you know your material down cold.

Master it first in your mind.

- Pay attention to your thoughts; become aware of the conversation in your head. Speak the words out loud, without filtering or editing, so you hear what that internal monologue is really saying.

- When you notice your thoughts going negative, stop and reframe. Sort out what you're currently thinking, and what positive thoughts you would replace it with. Write this out, if it helps. Give yourself positive language to frame what you want to see yourself doing: connecting bat and ball, as opposed to avoiding the strikeout.

- Hone those positive thoughts like a razor, so they send a clear signal to every part of your nervous and endocrine systems. See yourself vividly walking through the sequence of actions you want to master. And focus on doing it *right*. Remember that mental rehearsal takes just as much discipline as physical, maybe more.

Start in your comfort zone, then stretch.

- Isolate the fundamental elements of the challenge, and practice those under relaxed conditions until they are accurate and complete.

- Now apply repetition and refinement, gradually ramping up in speed, volume, scale, or whatever aspect or parameter you need to increase.

- Push the limits. Floor it! When you start losing accuracy, scale back again to within your competence zone until you have it fully back under control. Then start pushing the limits again. Take it as far as you can—and then 5 percent further.

- In other words: start within the limitations of your current competence and then build on that. *Crawl, walk, run.*

Raise the bar.

- Rehearse more than you think you need to. Don't practice for what you expect to do, practice for that times ten. Overprepare.

■ Come up with unlikely scenarios and prepare for those, too. Think of ten different ways it could go wrong, then practice how you would deal with all ten situations. Prepare for what *could* happen but probably never will. Because it might.

■ Constantly raise your standards of rehearsal. Training never stops. Challenge yourself. Never settle. Embrace excellence.

3

LETTING GO

Today is a good day to die.

—CRAZY HORSE,
before the Battle of the Little Bighorn

I'D BEEN OUT of the service for more than five years, most of that time spent building Wind Zero, my multimillion-dollar business venture. I'd poured in just about all my net worth, money I'd been saving for years, as well as money from a lot of investors, including family members, friends from the military, and more. All this had blown up in my face.

And then my wife told me she was leaving. And taking the kids.

There are fears like the fear of falling, of flying, of injury and death. For me, none of those is very strong. You can talk about bombs and bullets all day long; drowning or being waterboarded, shot in the Afghan high-mountain desert, thrown to rot in an Iraqi prison. True, none of that sounds very appealing. But this was worse. The situation I was in now played on my deepest, darkest fear.

Fear of total personal failure.

I'd lost my business, our life savings, and now my family. *Three strikes and you're out.*

Keeping this family together was the reason I'd left the military in the first place. There was nothing in the world more important to me than our kids. We were never going to be *that* family, the one that split up and fractured our kids' lives. Yet here it was, staring me in the face. *What?*

Not that it was entirely out of the blue. The marriage had seen its troubles, especially with me being away so much during the sniper school years. But we'd stuck together through the tough times, and I'd thought we were in a pretty good place. That maybe we'd weathered the fire. We'd just signed a lease on a new place. The school year was about to start. I was going to coach Little League.

I thought of Gene Hackman's last line in that Clint Eastwood masterpiece *Unforgiven*. Hackman plays Little Bill Daggett, the corrupt sheriff Eastwood guns down. As he lies dying, in disbelief at his own mortality, he says, "I don't deserve this, to die like this. I was building a house. . . ."

That was me, in disbelief at my own fallibility. *I was building a family. . . .*

Sitting broke and alone in a brand-new and very empty apartment, I had sober thoughts about a quick hop off the

Coronado Bridge. Discarded that idea pretty quick, though: couldn't do that to my kids. Besides, my life was just getting going; I wanted to be around to see how the whole story ends.

Next thought, my fallback position: reenlist. Would the service take me back? Of course. But I've never been much for the easy path, or for going backward. Discarded that one just as fast. So then . . . what? I could keep sitting there in my house and hold on to the shame, wallow in the failure. Get drunk, maybe? Call a friend and have a feel-sorry-for-myself marathon?

Or I could let go of all that and face the reality of the situation.

I let go, picked up the phone, and started dealing with the mess.

Pulling out of the wreckage that was my life, I negotiated out of our lease and got myself into a small apartment I could afford. I made some calls, asked around, and managed to find a high-paying job in the defense industry, which I clung to like driftwood. Started paying back some family and friends who'd invested in my failed business and getting my feet back on the ground.

In the course of digging out, I began looking at all the positives I had going for me. Three great kids, all healthy. An ex-wife who was willing to work with me and take the high road. And a great job.

The defense company I now worked for put me in charge

of running a division, managing a classified program with SOCOM (Special Operations Command), helping make sure that the engineers who were building radios and algorithms and other comms equipment for our Spec Ops forces weren't spending millions of dollars building things the teams would use as paperweights. Lisa, the VP I reported to, was a fantastic leader and excellent mentor, someone I looked up to and admired. I was dealing in elevated circles and making connections that could easily facilitate an upward career path. It was work that made a difference. And I was earning nearly two hundred grand a year. In so many ways, it was perfect.

So why, a few months in, was I thinking of leaving the job and starting another business?

"Are you out of your *freaking mind*?" my friends said. "You've got a fantastic job with lucrative pay and benefits and excellent upwardly mobile prospects! There are tons of people who would kill to have what you have! And you're going to unhook yourself from that phenomenal professional and financial life-support system to strike out on your own again, and launch *yet another start-up*? When the smoke has barely cleared from your last disaster?"

I had to admit, they had a point. A number of points, in fact, and they were all good ones. But none of them was the *key* point.

The job was great. But it was a coconut.

SOMETIMES YOU HAVE TO
LET GO OF THE COCONUT

A friend of mine from the Philippines tells me how they trap monkeys in his country. They dig a hole, place a coconut in it; the monkey reaches in, grabs the coconut, and his fist is now too big to pull back out. He's trapped. All he has to do is let go of the coconut. But he won't do it. Why not? What keeps that monkey's fist clenched? Fear. He's afraid of losing what he has. So he keeps the coconut—and loses his freedom.

I did not want to keep the coconut and lose my freedom.

What kept Kamal adhered to that poolside wall on the first day of our swim lessons? What prevents people from taking the risks they need to take in order to achieve the things they dream of achieving? What keeps people stuck in relationships that aren't working, in dead-end jobs they hate, or even, as in my case, in *great* jobs that nonetheless are holding them back from something that could be even better? They can't let go of the coconut.

You can achieve great things.

But first you have to let go of the coconut.

Mastering fear starts with a decision, then proceeds through rehearsal, so that you'll be as prepared as possible to make that jump into the unknown and take action in the face of your fear. But nine times out of ten, when the time comes to make the jump, something keeps people from actually doing it. Something they're holding on to.

For Kamal, it was the edge of the pool. In our life journey it's called "home." Before you can take that leap into the unknown of your adult life, you have to leave childhood behind, cut the apron strings, kick away the training wheels. You have to leave home. You have to let go.

Letting go is where you relinquish control, release your grip on the door frame before jumping out of the plane. It's where you step away from the ladder and walk out to the end of the high-dive board, take a breath, and stand there without visible means of support.

I stepped away from the ladder, out to the end of the high-dive board, and took a breath. Let go of that fantastic defense job and dove into another start-up.

Within a few years I was turning down a $15 million acquisition offer and well on my way toward having a company worth ten times that number. Rather than crashing and burning, this time the business was a flaming success. Worth the leap? Hell, yes. But none of it could have happened if I hadn't first let go of the coconut.

UNDERSTAND THAT SAFETY IS AN ILLUSION

One reason fear can get its grip on us, perhaps the biggest reason of all, is that it speaks directly to our natural impulse for self-preservation. Fear is awareness of danger, right? And naturally, you want to keep yourself safe, correct? Ah, but that's a trap! And within that trap is a secret, one that might be uncomfortable to hear but will liberate you if you let it:

You're never safe.

The trap is simply this: If you think you can achieve and maintain genuine safety, then you'll never risk anything. And you'll never really live.

The liberation is this: once you understand that complete safety will forever be out of your reach, it frees you to embrace those risks that are worth it, and to do so with passion and abandon.

It might seem like SEALs have a devil-may-care, screw-it approach to safety. In fact, the opposite is true. As I've mentioned, we are fanatical about training and preparation. We actually place a huge value on safety. But we also know its limits. We know that when it comes right down to it, *safety is an illusion.*

Kamal's first career was in trauma research. For four years, he got up every day and went to work until late at night in a level-one trauma center, where he would wait for the people who would soon be trucked in all mangled up from whatever serious accident had just happened, so he could collect data and take samples.

"I watched a lot of people die," he says. "And these were people who woke up that morning just like everyone else, shaved, got in the car, and went off to work, just like any other day. Except that this particular day ended with them lying on a gurney surrounded by their crying family."

As much as we work to build in a framework of consistency and familiarity, we will never change the bedrock fact that life is entirely unpredictable. It's entropy, the second law of thermodynamics: all orderly systems will eventually break down and turn to hydrogen. The other day some guy took a truck screaming down a bike path on New York's West Side, plowing down joggers and pedestrians, hitting as many people as he could. Killed eight and injured twenty more. I easily could have been there. It was just blocks from where I live. And hey, it doesn't take an act of terrorism. I take my dog out walking the street, I'm on the phone, distracted, he's pulling on the leash, a cabbie happens to take the wrong left that morning and—*boom!* I'm gone.

It happens. It happens every day.

So we do what we can to tilt the odds in favor of our safety, well-being, and continued longevity, yet ultimately we have no genuine control over the outcome. Does safety matter? Of course. As long as you understand that in the big picture, there is no such thing.

And if safety is an illusion, then what's the point of playing life as a spectator, watching from the stands? Sitting up on the bleachers is no safer than being right out on the field. Even if you opt to play it safe and avoid taking all risks, you can't, because that option does not in fact exist. "Playing it safe" is a fool's fantasy.

I say this because it puts fear in a different perspective. Much of what gives our fears their power over us, what keeps us clinging to the side and holds us back from jumping into the deep end of the pool, is our impulse to hang on to where we are, to what we know, to "what has always worked before" and "the way things have always been." But it's no safer over here than it is over there.

Every great gain, for humanity as a whole or for you or me in our own lives, has come about only through risk. Taking that job you weren't sure you could handle; letting go of that other job for a new opportunity. Joining the service. Leaving the service. Asking that girl to dance. Opening your own business. Hell, just coming down the birth canal and out into this bright, noisy world was a terrifying risk. It was safe and quiet in there!

But the risk is worth it, because there's that ring, that treasure, those keys to the kingdom, that heart's desire at the end of the path.

Another great line from cinema history: Butch and Sundance are on the run from the super-posse and reach a cliff, a raging river way down below. No way out; the only choice is to jump. But Sundance won't do it. Butch presses him. Sundance refuses. Finally he blurts out, "I can't swim!"

Butch looks at him and says, "You crazy bastard. The *fall*'ll probably kill ya."

So sure, you *could* stay up here on the cliff where it's "safe," and wait for the super-posse to come take you away to prison. Or you could jump. What's that? You're afraid you may not be able to swim? Refer to *Cassidy, Butch.*

TUNE OUT THE BULLSHIT

I have a friend, Chris Ward, who joined the marines after graduating from high school in the early eighties. Chris loved music and was a huge fan of the Ramones, the legendary punk rock band. He loved their take-no-prisoners style. If the Marine Corps ethic could be put into rock and roll, it would look and sound a lot like the Ramones.

Then, in the summer of 1989, when Chris was near the end of his tour, the group's bass player, Dee Dee Ramone, quit the band. Chris couldn't believe it. Bass was Chris's instrument; Dee Dee was his favorite band member. He ranted about it to a marine buddy. "This is *bullshit*, man—it ain't the Ramones without Dee Dee!" And he swore he'd never go to another Ramones show.

As it turned out, he was wrong. He did go to a few more Ramones shows.

All of them, in fact.

When he heard that the Ramones were auditioning for a new bass player, Chris tried out (after two days straight of round-the-clock practicing) and son of a bitch: *he landed the gig.* To join the band, he had to change his name. None of the band members were born with the name Ramone; they *all* took on stage names. So Christopher Joseph Ward ceased being Christopher Joseph Ward—and became C. J. Ramone.

C.J.'s first event was booked for five weeks to the day after he left the marines. Which meant he had thirty-five days to learn and rehearse forty songs. He lived in his room for those five weeks and did nothing but play bass. He ate dinner sitting with his bass. He slept with his bass. He practiced and practiced and practiced. When the night came, he stood in the wings, trying to prepare himself to step out onstage and actually *become* a Ramone. To take the place of one of the most legendary bass players and songwriters in rock-and-roll history. But all he could hear were his own words in his head:

"This is *bullshit,* man—it ain't the Ramones without Dee Dee!"

Johnny Ramone, the guitarist and one of the band's founders, looked him dead in the eyes and said, "You ready to go?" It was terrifying. He felt like he was going to throw up. In that moment, C.J. says, he knew he had to make a choice. He could stay trapped in the bullshit. Or he could let it go.

He took a breath and stepped out onto the stage with the others.

People in the crowd booed him, yelled at him, threw bottles and boots and all sorts of crap at him. People spit on him. There were a few standing right up front holding a sign that said "WE WANT DEE DEE," screaming and cursing at him. One girl, sitting up on her boyfriend's shoulders, gave him the finger.

But none of that mattered. C.J.'s biggest detractor was the voice in his own head saying, *This is bullshit, man!*—and he'd already stopped listening.

He played every show until the group disbanded in 1996.

Sometimes the bullshit is your own internal monologue talking, as it was for C.J. Sometimes it's the people around you—even those you're closest to.

You've probably had that experience, of people who love you urging you *not* to do that thing that your heart is telling you to do. It's not easy, is it? Because you don't want to ignore the voice of experience. You don't want to do something foolish, something you'll later regret. But there are times when people close to you say, "Don't do it!"—and your gut says, *Do it!* I know I've certainly had that experience, more than once.

So has my friend Maria Emma.

Maria is phenomenally talented—competition figure skater, art prodigy, a whiz at people management, and a voracious entrepreneur. By age sixteen she was running two nationally top-rated skating rinks, with forty coaches and four hundred students. She became the youngest freshman ever to enroll at the Fashion Institute of Technology. At eighteen she took a management position with Walmart, and within six months was hiring and firing and being accountable for $15 billion in apparel. At which point she decided to go into business for herself with a design franchise opportunity called EmbroidMe. She bought the franchise for Manhattan.

And everyone told her it wouldn't work.

Like me, when my friends told me I was crazy to leave my defense job, Maria had to admit: they had a point. This was 2008. The nation's economy was in meltdown mode. She'd just left an amazing, high-paying job, she'd poured everything she had into this new business (some $300,000, by the time she hung out her shingle), the economy was crashing, she was living on ramen noodles and running her little retail operation out of her tiny studio apartment, a sixth-floor walk-up on Thirty-fourth Street, because that was all she could afford. Five hundred square feet: basically, Maria and a desk. Customers had to buzz up to be let in.

"Are you crazy?" her friends said. "Nobody's going to come up to the sixth floor!"

So she made one of the most excruciating decisions of her life.

To close the business? Accept defeat? No—to cut ties, at least for the moment, with those friends and family who were telling her it wouldn't work. That night she sat in her car, broke down, and cried.

"It was incredibly painful," says Maria. "But necessary." She knew that if she spent too much time around them, hearing their constant doubts would make her walls start crumbling. What made this especially hard to do was that Maria knew there was some truth in what they were all saying. But she didn't want to buy into that story line.

"For me," says Maria, "fear has zero percent to do with

your circumstance, and one hundred percent to do with your mindset. Was I afraid? Of course! But I decided to look at the fear as an invitation to dive in and write a new story line." We'll revisit Maria's story in chapter 5, but here's the short version: the business became a smash success.

Sometimes the static comes from well-meaning friends, as in Maria's case. Sometimes it comes from unhappy, mean-spirited people who are *trying* to take you down.

The last few years, there's been a little clique of disgruntled former SEALs who have followed my career and heckled me constantly, telling anyone who will listen that I'm a fraud and posting smack talk about me on social media. It's like having a bunch of groupies, only in reverse. (I love what Paulo Coelho says about this: "Haters are confused admirers.")

For a few years, it got to me, and I would try to fight it. Then one day I asked myself: If I sat down in my doctor's office tomorrow and he said, "Webb, you're dying, you've got a year left," would I care about what some disaffected people are saying about me on social media? Of course not. I'd be on the phone lining up the flights for a yearlong trip with my kids. I'd spend every moment of that one remaining year with my family and friends, making great memories, pouring myself into the things that matter most.

Of course, the doctor hasn't said that, not to me and probably not to you, either. But whether it's one year left or fifty years left, what's the difference? No life span is long enough to justify wasting a day of it listening to the bullshit. There will always be critics, always people who want to rain on your parade, bring you down, steal your dreams, or stop you from leaping forward. You can listen and believe it if you want. Or you can let go of it all and tune in to what's important.

WHEN OPPORTUNITY COMES, GRAB IT

After recounting his story on my podcast, C. J. Ramone made an observation that stayed with me.

"Real opportunity is a rare thing," he said. "I see friends who want to start a business or make some other big move in their lives, and I tell them, 'Stop thinking you have to keep prepping. You know you want to do it. You've already made up your mind. There's no more prepping. You just have to take the chance, and *go*.'"

There comes a point where it's no longer about prep—it's about taking a chance.

You've probably heard this one: "Opportunity is everywhere you look, if you just keep your eyes open." It's not really true. I never hear genuinely successful entrepreneurs say that, because they know that *real* opportunity, the kind you can grab on to and take for a ride around the world, is a rare and valuable thing. It isn't something you'll find lying around on every street corner.

C.J. is right on. Opportunity is *not* everywhere you look. It comes—but very, very seldom. And when it does, too many people blow the chance to jump on it because they're too busy feeling they're not ready yet, that they're not prepared enough.

This was something we saw again and again in the sniper course. We would do stalking exercises, where students would have to sneak up to within two hundred meters of two instructors and then, once they were in place, set up for a shot. The instructors, meanwhile, would be watching carefully, doing their best to catch a glimpse of the stalking students. If you were seen, that was a fail.

We also had walkers in the field, out among the students, whose job it was to watch the students but not give away their location. I spent quite a bit of time both as one of the target instructors and as a walker. I would watch these guys take two or three hours to creep up to the two-hundred-meter zone—and then spend another hour prepping. Granted, it takes a while to get everything set up just right, to make sure you have a clean sight line and shot line and that your concealment is perfect, so that when you finally take the shot there won't be any telltale movements of a stray leaf or obvious powder flash.

So, yeah, it takes a while. But not an *hour*.

Yet some guys would lie there forever, prepping and prepping . . . and never take that shot. Eventually the clock would run out and they would fail the stalk without ever pulling the trigger. The problem wasn't the logistics of the shot itself. They knew how to do that. They had it down. The problem was, they couldn't let go of the prep phase.

I see this a lot in my civilian life, too. People who get stuck in their jobs, their careers, or whatever their present circumstances are, preparing, preparing, saying "Now's not the time," or "It doesn't feel right yet," or "I'm not quite ready yet."

Please, don't make the same mistake. Don't miss out on what could be the greatest experiences and opportunities of your life because you feel you're "not ready." I think this tragic mistake stems from a misunderstanding of the word "ready." *Ready* does not mean you've removed all uncertainty. It doesn't mean you've practiced to the point where what comes next will be *easy*. It won't be easy. No leap worth taking is easy.

All *ready* means is you've suited up and mounted your horse. Now it's time to ride.

C.J. hit the nail on the head. Our time on this planet is so limited and so precious. Truly great opportunities are scarce. You have to be prepared to seize on them when they come, and the lion's share of that preparation is pure mindset. You have to be practiced at letting go—and willing to take the shot.

GET OUT OF THE ECHO CHAMBER

I've told you about Kamal's fear of being underwater and his lifelong inability (until recently) to swim. What we haven't yet touched on is . . . why?

As it turns out, there is a very concrete answer. When Kamal was just four years old, he fell into a swampy bog and sank. The only reason he didn't drown was that someone happened to see him fall in and waded in after him. His memory of the event is hazy. In fact, incredibly, he had completely forgotten about it until we started talking about his fear of swimming in the course of working on this book.

Sometimes the fear that holds us back has nothing directly to do with present circumstances. Sometimes what's happening right now resonates so strongly with past events that it evokes deep layers of response and reaction. The great majority of the fears most of us experience day to day are nothing but shadowboxing: not a response to a genuine danger but a reaction to the reverberations of events long behind us.

For example, that business failure I went through in 2011. What made that so devastating? Of course any male ego hates the idea of failing. To a Navy SEAL, it's ten times worse. But there was more to it than that. There was something personal about it.

When I was six years old, my dad's construction business failed. I remember it vividly, even though I didn't fully grasp what was going on at the time. It's not that I saw *him* as a failure. I didn't, and don't. And it's not that the experience diminished him in my eyes. But the whole tone of our lives changed. We moved, then moved again. I started getting in more fights. For our family it was the end of an era, and the start of a new, much more uncertain, and far less happy one.

Fast-forward about thirty years to the collapse of Wind Zero and that empty, silent apartment. To me, I suppose, "business failing" meant more than simply losing my savings. In the echo chamber, it telegraphed a message that went something like this: *And now, the family suffers.* And sure enough, the next thing I knew, my wife and three kids were moving to another state.

Pulling out of that cloud of despair meant I had to shake off all the implications and connotations of what was happening and get myself back into the here and now. Sure, I could have gone into a repeating tape loop of what went wrong, of whose fault it was, who did what and when and to whom, an endless hamster wheel of scorekeeping, and kept that drama spinning for years. People do it all the time. And to what end?

The truth was, my wife and I still had a solid connection, and we were both determined to give our kids the most stable, healthy growing-up experience we possibly could. And we have. We've never let the breakup of our marriage rip open a gaping separation between the kids and either one of us. Ever since that fall I've been in their lives constantly. My ex and I have stayed on great terms; she eventually remarried an excellent guy, and I'm on great terms with him as well. We may not have succeeded at marriage, but I'll tell you what, we've done as good a job with *family* as any divorced couple I've ever known.

But for all that good stuff to unfold, I first had to get out of the echo chamber.

Every one of us lives in our own private echo chamber. What's in yours?

Perhaps you were teased in school. Abused at home, physically or verbally, by a parent or older sibling. Maybe you've done things you're not proud of, or had things done to you that you can't forgive. Could be you were traumatized by events that had nothing to do with you, but which you had the misfortune to witness, and are still carrying around with you today. For example, say your parents used to have violent fights when you were a kid. Now every time you sense the hint of a difference of opinion, you blanch, feint, and evade. It's got nothing to do with today's disagreement—you're ducking to avoid a fight that was over and done with thirty years ago.

Whatever's in it, one thing is for sure: you've got an echo chamber and the internal monologue that goes with it. Everyone does.

Wartime veterans, of course, often experience an echo chamber of an especially hellish kind.

On my *Power of Thought* podcast I interviewed a true "greatest generation" hero, Captain Jerry Yellin. Jerry enlisted in the army on his eighteenth birthday, just a few months after Pearl Harbor, and ended up landing on Iwo Jima as part of the 78th Fighter Squadron. Eight square miles of land, where 67,000 U.S. Marines fought against 23,000 Japanese. There were some 28,000 bodies rotting in the sun, 21,000 Japanese and nearly 7,000 marines.

"When I landed, I smelled the smell of death," Jerry said, "and it never left me."

A month later he flew the first long-range Air Corps mission over Japan. Incredibly, he also ended up flying the *last* combat mission of the war. Sixteen of the young men he flew with didn't come home.

When Jerry got home from the war, he fell into a dark hole. As he tells it, he was a basket case for the next thirty years. He couldn't work, couldn't function, couldn't talk about his wartime experiences. Couldn't understand why he had survived when so many of his buddies did not. Despite having a wife he loved and four beautiful boys, Jerry couldn't find his way out of the echo chamber and back to the land of the living. And so it went for thirty years, depressed, lonely, and hopeless.

In 1975, he learned about meditation, and in a matter of months his sense of life began to wake up again. Now he travels the world sharing his story and working to bring healing and hope to a new generation of veterans who are battling post-traumatic stress.

Jerry found his way out through meditation. That's one way. Another is to go ski Mont Blanc.

In 2017 I took four Spec Ops vets and a camera crew on a five-day ski trip to Chamonix, France, and up the back of Mont Blanc, the highest peak in the Alps, to shoot a documentary titled *Big Mountain Heroes,* about veterans transitioning to civilian life. A lot of these men and women have seen and experienced terrible things, memories they can't shake and struggles they can't process with anyone who wasn't there. There are plenty of proven and promising alternative therapies out there, but the VA typically throws pills at the problem, which only creates a cycle of addiction and victimization. We need to be looking for ways to *empower* these returning heroes, not to sedate them.

That was our mission in Chamonix. "Thrills before pills," we called it.

"We'll never be fully healed," says one of the guys in the documentary. "But every time we stepped outside, we put one more stitch in the wound."

The echo chamber's grip is not necessarily about post-traumatic stress, or even about past trauma. Often it's simply a sort of hypernostalgia that keeps you in its clutches—and away from engaging in your present reality. I've seen a lot of guys who've separated from the service technically, but they're still living there in their heads, surrounding themselves with memorabilia of their time overseas, spending all their free time only with other vets and nobody outside that sacred circle. It's as if the only way they can justify their existence is by leaning on their identity as former military guys. They're like those dads who constantly talk about their college glory days, the implication always being that their best is behind them and life is all downhill from here.

There's nothing wrong with cherishing fond memories, just as there can be a lot to gain from sorting through past hardships and pain for perspectives that may serve us in the present day. The problem comes when you get trapped in that place. One more hamster on the wheel.

When you find that happening to you, there's only one thing to do. Flip the switch. Change the conversation in your head. Let the past be in the past. And while we're at it, let the future be in the future.

Engage in the present.

LEARN HOW TO DIE

When I started my *Power of Thought* podcast, my very first guest was James Altucher. James is one of the most amazing guys I've ever known. He started out in the eighties as a computer programmer, wrote his first code on an Apple II in 1982. In the early nineties he predicted that every company would eventually need a website, and of course, people thought he was crazy. He started one of the first website services, building sites for such clients as American Express, Disney, Miramax, Sony, and Time Warner. When he sold his website business in 1998 he pocketed some $15 million.

But he was, as he puts it, "young and stupid," and within less than four years, through a series of poor investments and bad decisions, he went from having millions in the bank to having a balance of less than $200. Suicide crossed his mind. "I thought my two little girls might be better off with the $4 million payout from my life insurance than with me," says James.

Instead, he put his bottomless curiosity to work. Starting with what he'd observed about buying and selling companies, he studied the investment world. He downloaded fifty years of stock data and spent hours doing statistical modeling. Became an investment guru. Started an investment newsletter and sold it to TheStreet.com for millions. Got involved in a mental health company and sold it for millions. Started more than a dozen other companies. Ran a hedge fund. Started one of the most popular podcasts on the planet. Wrote more than a dozen books, one of which was named by USA Today as "one of the twelve best business books of all time."

Somewhere in that timeline, he lost everything a second time, then built it all back up again. And then a third time.

James is constantly pushing himself to do new and challenging things. But this year he did something nobody saw coming. A very shy guy, James had a massive fear of public speaking. So what did he do? He decided to do stand-up comedy. And not just anywhere. He wanted to take his act to a prominent club in Manhattan.

"I was scared to death," he says. To which I say, *No shit*.

If you think the idea of speaking in public is terrifying, imagine being a stand-up comic. Stand-ups not only have to speak in front of a crowd, they have to make the audience laugh. And do it over and over, moment after moment after moment, without fail. Because as every pro comic knows, your act can go into a nosedive in a matter of seconds, and when it does, it's tougher to pull out than a single-engine plane in a hurricane. In fact, the experience of having your act go south is so common, so universal, that comedians have a term for it.

They call it *dying onstage*.

Twice a week, James goes to a club somewhere in Manhattan and does stand-up comedy. I've been to hear his show. He's actually pretty funny. And talk about cojones. The other day, to help tighten up his one-liners, he went down into the subway with a video crew and did a little stand-up at each stop, all the way from Twenty-eighth Street down to the Brooklyn Bridge.

How can he possibly *do* that?

I think I know the answer. James has already died, not once but several times. He has lost everything, rebuilt it out of thin air, then lost it again, and rebuilt it out of thin air again. He has reinvented himself so many times he's become like a cat with *ninety-nine* lives.

Here is one of his secrets: He has a daily discipline, a mental checklist that includes "taking ownership of whatever happens to me." He doesn't allow himself to blame anyone or anything, just owns it as his life, his circumstance, the way he's created it at this moment—and then asks himself, "Okay, what's next?"

I opened this chapter with that famous quote from Crazy Horse, the Lakota warrior who led his people to victory in the Battle of the Little Bighorn. "Today is a good day to die." Why? Because the sun is in the sky, the earth is abundant beneath my feet, and I'm breathing rich air in and out of my lungs. I'm living in the present moment, which is to say, I'm grounded in eternity. No regrets for the past, no worries for the future. Sun, ground, air: just life, as it is. As good a time to die as any.

AND DIE OFTEN

So we've talked about death, but let's really *talk* about it. Let's put it right out on the table.

You're going to die.

That's just how it is. You're going to die. And I know you know that. We all know it—in theory. But until you *really* know it, know it with your cells, in your gut, with every breath, until death is real and your own impermanence is a concrete, ever-present, palpable thing, then death is still lurking unseen, whispering its threats and taunting you from the shadows. Which means death still has mastery over you. To live a rich life, you need it to be the other way around.

You need to have mastery over death.

Why? That's a reasonable question. After all, if death doesn't come till the end, then why should it matter today how you greet it when it eventually comes? The answer is that death *isn't* something that comes only at the end. It's with you from the moment you're born. It's hovering over you right now.

And isn't that what lies at the heart of so many of our most common fears? Not just the obvious ones—fear of heights, fear of flying, fear of the dark—but so many others, too, that don't seem to be connected to death in any obvious way.

Earlier I posed the question: In the fear of public speaking, what are we really afraid of? What's the danger there? The worst that can happen is that we'll look foolish. As John Cleese says, "It is the goal of every Englishman to make it all the way to his grave without becoming embarrassed." But isn't that embarrassment a pre-echo of our own impending demise? "Dying onstage" may not mean dying literally, but it is a death of sorts—a death to our self-image, self-esteem, and ego. To our sense of safety and identity.

"The obsessive need to be right," writes Eckhart Tolle in *The Power of Now,* "is an expression of the fear of death." And what is the obsessive need to be right but an obsessive fear of being wrong? To me, the ability to freely admit you were wrong is the beginning of mature adulthood. To do it, you have to be willing to die a little.

When I was starting Hurricane, a wealthy friend told me something about investment: you should always invest, he said, only the amount you are prepared to lose. I believe you can't be a truly, hugely successful entrepreneur unless you are prepared to lose *everything*, like James Altucher. It's no accident that the average millionaire has been through three or four bankruptcies.

We have a saying in the military: when you enlist you write a blank check made payable to the United States of America for an amount "up to and including your life." This is what a lot of Spec Ops training is all about. You come face-to-face with your own mortality, and not just once, but over and over, like Bill Murray in *Groundhog Day*. You die dozens of times, and keep going each time, knowing that one of these fine days, you'll die and stay dead—and that until that day, you are *alive*.

To master fear, you have to let go of the illusion of safety, which really means letting go of the illusion of immortality. The truth is, at some point you will die, and you don't know when, so you have to be ready right now—so you can take a breath, and *live*.

By "die often," I mean develop the practice of stopping

everything you're doing for a moment and asking yourself, "If I died, right now, this minute, would I be okay with that?"

If we're honest with ourselves, often the answer is "No!" Because there are too many problems we haven't solved, ambitions still unfulfilled, dreams still unchased, too much about our lives that we haven't figured out or had the chance to explore and enjoy yet. We're caught up with the unresolved past and the uncertain future. We're like St. Augustine, who as a young man prayed to God: "Lord, make me chaste—but not yet!"

As you master your fears, you'll find that, like Crazy Horse, you can ask that question, "If I died today, would I be okay with that?" and answer truthfully: "Yes. It's not my plan or my intention or my preference—but if I died right now, this minute? So be it."

And then add: "Meanwhile, here I am!"

PRACTICE POINTS

Once you have prepared as much as possible, there comes a point when you have to let go of whatever crutch, limitation, or safety blanket you've been holding on to that keeps you from diving in. You have to relinquish control, cut the apron strings, kick away the training wheels. To let go of the coconut.

When opportunity comes, seize it.

- Don't get stuck in endless prep. Understand that practice and rehearsal can take you only so far; don't let "I'm still getting ready" become an excuse for failing to take action when the situation presents itself. You'll *never* be fully "ready."

- Tune out the bullshit, whether it's coming from yourself, your friends, or detractors. Don't fight it or respond to it; just tune it out, period.

Get out of the echo chamber.

- Examine your fear. Is it about a challenge directly in front of you, in the here and now, or is it in reaction to events long behind you? Are you shadowboxing with the distant past?

- If your fear is about a clear and present danger, then *flip the switch* and focus on what positive actions you can take to meet the challenge.

- If it is a pattern of reaction to echoes of the past, then identify that—write it down if it helps—and let it go. And *then* focus on positive action. Let the past be in the past, the future in the future, and engage in the present.

Embrace mortality.

- Let go of the illusion of safety, security, identity, ego, and immortality.

- Imagine that in this instant your life is suddenly over. Your consciousness is hovering over your dead body, looking down, reviewing the situation. How do you feel about it? Are you basically okay with the life you lived? Or do you feel strong regrets, and if so, what are they?

- Returning to your real life in the present moment, what steps can you take to engage and eliminate those regrets?

- Repeat this exercise often, until you find yourself at the point where you can honestly say, yes, if you died today, right now, you could look back and say, "I'm good."

4

JUMPING OFF

Optimism, pessimism, fuck that;
we're going to make it happen.

—Elon Musk,
on his goal to put a rocket into orbit

WHATEVER JOURNEY YOU'RE on, there comes a point where you have to untie the boat and go. Sign the contract, make the announcement, tell your toxic partner that it's over. Whatever it is, in your situation, it's the action that takes you past the point of no return. The second hand reaches twelve, the buzzer goes off. It's time to jump, and when that happens, there's only one thing to do.

Jump.

You can't reason your way into this step or self-coach your way through it. You can't intellectualize it. Panic comes from the brain stem, and you can't talk things over with your brain stem. It's got to be visceral. It's about taking action.

If you wait for the fear to go away first, you'll never do it.

Because the fear is never going away. There comes a moment, though, when the fear crystallizes into a kind of stark clarity. When you suddenly see an opening, like a quarterback spotting a hole in the defensive line where he can run for the touchdown, or a performer backstage hearing the sudden hush seconds before the curtain goes up.

It's that moment the universe realigns itself around you and whispers in your ear, "It's time." And gives you a nudge in the ass.

ONE OF MY toughest encounters with fear hit me in the face at twelve thousand feet, when they told me it was my turn to jump out of the plane.

It was 2004; I'd already been through two deployments, including six months in Afghanistan right after 9/11. By this time I was back stateside, running the SEAL sniper program with Eric Davis. Because of a fluke in scheduling, there was one essential training that I'd missed during my original SEAL training workup years earlier: high-altitude parachute jump, also known as "military freefall."

This should not have been a problem. As a kid, I was born with that same daredevil gene that everyone in Spec Ops seems to have. I was always climbing, jumping off heights, doing insanely risky things, driving my mom to the edge. She once got so frazzled trying to rein me in and protect me from my own wildness that she called Social Services and told the lady on the other end of the phone that her two-year-old son was driving her so nuts, she was afraid she was about to hurt him. (Sorry, Mom.)

What's more, I *loved* being in the air. For as long as I could remember, I'd always wanted to become a pilot. My earliest memory is of my mother forcing my dad to take me to see *Star Wars* when it first came out. I was three. He said it was "sci-fi bullshit" and wanted no part of it. After taking me to see it, he went back himself and watched it again five times. (You're welcome, Dad.) By 2004 I'd taken courses at Embry-Riddle Aeronautical University and would soon be getting my pilot's license.

So what was the problem?

The problem was that I'd had a bad experience with high-altitude jumps. When I went through SEAL sniper school in 2000, there was a guy in our class, Mike Bearden, whom we all looked up to. He was one of the nicest guys I'd ever met, and a total stud, just crushed every exercise, every drill, every standard. We called him "the Bear." A few weeks after sniper school ended, Mike went out for military freefall training, where they'd be jumping out of planes at ten thousand to twelve thousand feet. On one of the last days of jump school, the Bear ran into any military trainer's worst nightmare: his main chute got tangled in his backup. He fought it all the way to the ground.

This was now four years later, and I'd been through a

good deal of wartime experience. But Bearden's death had brought up a bone-deep fear that stayed with me, and would continue to stay with me until I faced it.

I knew it was nothing but that hamster on the wheel, that story running in my head. Still, it wasn't entirely a made-up story, right? I mean, Bearden was practically a god to us: not only an ouststanding performer but an outstanding human being. If there was anyone who ever *least* deserved to die before his time, it was Mike.

But it happened. And if it happened to Mike, who was to say it wouldn't happen to me?

All this ran through my mind as our little twin-engine climbed to twelve thousand feet, more than two miles above the earth's surface. I was ready for this, I told myself. I'd trained for it. I'd done plenty of low-altitude jumps. I knew what I was doing.

But still.

Another guy in our jump class, when he saw that rear ramp door open, got right back into his seat, his back to the plane wall, and buckled himself in. "The hell with that shit," he said. As I stepped around the guy and over to the open door, I wondered what was going through his mind. Had he never really *made the decision,* like so many of my former BUD/S classmates who dropped out? Did he have some dark memory circulating in his own echo chamber? I would never know. Whatever the reason, though, one look at his face told me all that mattered: he had let the fear clutch at him and wrestle him to the floor. No jumping for him today. Or ever, most likely.

I felt that fear clutch at me, too, big-time, but instead of letting it freeze me, I grabbed at it and made it my fuel. Because I was ready. I'd decided. I'd prepared. And I had let go of the coconut.

I jumped.

MAKE A HABIT OF ASKING FOR WHAT YOU WANT

Not that "jumping off" is always as dramatic as leaping out of an airplane at twelve thousand feet. Sometimes it's as simple as asking for help.

I recently got into a conversation with an Uber driver who was taking me to the airport. I asked him how he liked his work. He started telling me all about it. He didn't want to be driving an Uber; there was so much more he wanted to do. He had so many great ideas. But there was this problem, and that barrier to entry, and some other thing in the way. He couldn't do this, couldn't do that. I zoned out on the details, but the message was clear: *I can't get ahead. And it's not my fault.*

"Hey, man," I said, "you ever hear of the SBA?"

No, he had no idea what that was.

I told him about the Small Business Administration, and

how they have this fantastic low-interest loan program for people in exactly his situation. How you can use a loan to buy or fund a business and be off and running in no time at all.

"Oh, my God," he said. "That's amazing! What's it called again? Can I email you? Can I reach out to you for the details?"

Now, I have not always been the most patient person. I've been working on changing that. I had a conversation with Jairek Robbins, Tony Robbins's son, and he said, "Hey, it's good to give a little time for up-and-comers, because you were there yourself once. Spend time with your peer group, and then push yourself to also devote a little time to people on their way up who are hungry to learn. That's a good mix."

What Jairek said sounded right and felt right. So I wanted to help this guy, this Uber driver. He was obviously smart. And it was clear that he was ambitious and had all kinds of ideas for ways he could get ahead in the world. There was no reason he couldn't make a success out of himself. And there was no reason I shouldn't help him do that.

I dug out my business card and gave it to him. Explained how to reach me. Told him to take me up on it, that I would definitely help him through the process. He took the card and thanked me profusely.

And you know what he did?

Absolutely nothing.

I never heard from him. Not a word. How many times has something like this happened to me? More times than I can count.

You reach a point where you have walked right up to the edge of the thing you want to have happen, and all you have to do, the only leap you need make, is to ask. No jumping out of airplanes, no diving off cliffs, no plunging into the water in the middle of the night. No getting up onstage and doing stand-up comedy, or speaking to a live audience of three million. All you need to do is say, "I want this. Will you help me?"

But you don't ask. You stand at the edge, mute, waiting for the door to open, but you don't knock. It's a tragedy. And it happens every day, in every city, millions of times a day.

That moment at the door is one of Kamal's yellow arrows, whispering, *"This way, this way . . ."* But instead of moving forward, you sit there waiting for the light to change. The light isn't going to change. *You* need to change.

The thing that made me sad about never hearing from the Uber driver was my sense that this was not the first time he'd been in this situation, nor would it be the last. Because whether you dare to make the move, or shrink from making the move, either way, it so quickly and so easily becomes habitual. When you reach that jumping-off point, whether you knock on the door or you don't, whether you call the number on the business card or you just let it sit in your glove compartment gathering dust, either way it has just become a part of how you operate. Over time, how you operate starts to become *who you are.* A habit of action or of nonaction, and before you know it, it adds up to a lifetime of exhilaration or disappointment, excellence or mediocrity, achievement or mere existence.

Daring to ask, or shrinking from asking: either way, it becomes a habit.

I heard a fantastic story from Jerry Yellin, my World War II fighter pilot friend, that was the polar opposite of the Uber driver story. When Jerry took his army entrance exams as a freshly minted eighteen-year-old, he passed the mental test easily but flunked the physical. The problem was his eyesight: he had 20/30 vision in one eye. He asked his mom, who was on the local draft board, if she could get him a copy of the eye chart. She did, and he memorized it, then went back and passed the eye exam.

He went through basic training, put in ten hours in a P-40, had his uniforms bought and all ready to go. Now all he had to do was take the final physical. When he got to the eye test, he found they'd changed the chart. He flunked. The doctor told him he'd done so well in training that they were going to graduate him anyway, and have him fly transports.

"Sir," said Jerry, "I'm a fighter pilot, I've got ten hours in a P-40. I'm not going to fly transports."

The doctor said, "You'll fly anything I tell you to fly."

Jerry asked, "Who can change that?"

"Only the commandant of cadets," the doc replied.

"How do I get to see him?"

"You go through the chain of command."

"What does that mean?"

"It means, you ask me first."

"Sir," said Jerry, "I want to see the commandant of cadets."

Next thing Jerry knew, he was standing in an office, saluting the commandant of cadets.

After Jerry explained his situation, the commandant said, "Son, anybody's got the guts to come to see me, you're a fighter pilot."

You want anything done, go to the person who can make that decision—and ask.

This happened to me multiple times in the military. When I wanted to try out for the SEAL program, the guy with the authority to approve my package turned it down. I had to wait six months, then resubmit—and this time, when he tried to sabotage me again, I went straight to his commanding officer. The package was approved. Years later, when Eric and I were running the sniper program and we had a boss who was wreaking havoc and sabotaging all our good work, I went over his head to the master chief in charge of the entire Naval Special Warfare Center, knowing that I was risking my entire military career doing it. Within twenty-four hours our boss was gone and I was put in charge. Sometimes you need to take the risk and ask for what you want.

Does that mean you're always going to get what you ask for? No. But if you *don't* ask, the odds of your getting it drop to roughly zero. And when you do ask, even if the answer is no, you're exercising your *jumping-off* muscles. Changing who you are.

And you don't need to be an aviator or a SEAL to do this. A thirteen-year-old girl can do it. I know, because I watched her.

My daughter wanted out of one of her classes in junior high. It wasn't that she didn't like the class, it was that she thought it was a waste of time. She did not bitch to her class-mates about it, or complain to her parents or Facebook friends about it. She sent an email directly to the school principal, telling him which class she wanted to leave, and why, and then specifying another class that she thought would be more valuable.

"This is the class I've identified," she wrote, "and I think I need to be transferred there."

The following semester, she got the transfer.

Where did she learn how to do that? I'll tell you where: from me. I've been teaching my kids this their whole lives: If you want it, you have to ask for it. Nobody else is going to do it for you.

Still, I don't think I would have had the balls to do that in eighth grade.

The other day we were at the Portland airport, having a meal while waiting to take a flight to go to my dad's wedding. As we sat there eating, my younger son Grayson said, "Oh, my God, that's my favorite player!" We looked over in the direc-tion where he'd nodded and saw the whole Portland Timbers soccer team sitting around a few tables, eating. The Timbers are a very big deal out there in the Northwest. Grayson was starstruck.

I sat back and watched as this conversation went down between Grayson and his siblings.

"Grayson," his older brother Hunter said, "you have to do this. If you want it, you've gotta ask for it."

"I'll go with you," added Olivia, "but you have to ask."

At that point I spoke up, too. "Look, buddy," I said, "you do what you want. But these opportunities don't come around very often."

He got up, went over to the first table, and asked. The whole team got up from their seats and stood around him to take a big group photo. You should have seen the smile on that kid's face. It was incredible to see the other two nudging him to go ask for it, and to watch him stand up and do it.

Now I'm nudging you: go ask for it.

HAVE FAITH IN THE ABYSS

What makes the jump so frightening is that you are relinquishing control, throwing yourself into the hands of the elements. Whether you are jumping out of a plane, leaving a job, entering into a new contract, or pushing out into the deep end of the pool, there is a sense of hurling yourself off a cliff and into the abyss. It can be terrifying.

Yet something amazing happens when you jump. If the decision gives you the courage, the jump gives you the power. You discover abilities in yourself that would not have shown up in a hundred years as long as you were still standing on the cliff hesitating.

It feels a little like entering a totally dark room and shutting the door behind you. Total blackness. You feel completely powerless and out of control. But you're *not* powerless or out of control, because as dark as the room seems, there *is* in fact a spark of light in there. Your job is to find it, and trust it.

There's a reason people call it a "leap of faith." You can plan and practice and rehearse, but there is always an element of letting go that releases you into the abyss where events unfold in a way that no training can fully predict or control, and this is the domain not of preparation but of faith. When you jump, you are heading into the abyss, and there's no solid ground in the abyss, no terra firma, nothing to stand on or hold on to, but faith.

Don't worry, I'm not going to get religious on you. This isn't about religion, or God, or any sort of particular spiritual viewpoint. It *is* about faith, though. You can't jump unless you have faith. In what?

In your training, for one thing. In the integrity and efficacy of your preparation. In your teachers, who helped you prepare. In yourself. You are ready for this. And sure, if you want: in God, in karma, in an outcome that serves the greater good. Whatever it is, find it and hold on to it.

Sometimes the only thing you can find to hold on to is a trust in your own decision. A great example is the stock market. The biggest reason most people don't make big money in the market is that they can't handle the abyss. When prices plummet, they panic and sell. But that is exactly when they should hold on and trust their original decision to buy that particular stock! Sure, it's scary when your stock price goes way down. But that's not the time to *sell*. That's the time to *buy*. The fear produced by the drop is not an alarm bell telling you "GET OUT! GET OUT!"—it's a signpost whispering, *"This way, this way,"* pointing the way to the prize.

When Kamal felt the panic of the abyss in our first few lessons, he wanted to sell out his stock and go grab the edge of the pool again. I showed him how to take a breath, flip over onto his back, and float. To get back to his happy place.

Having faith within the abyss, amid the panic of the plunge: that's your happy place.

When Hemingway felt too intimidated to write, he would say to himself, "You've written before, you know how to do it, sit down and write one true sentence—just one true sentence." Then he would write down one true sentence. The unwritten novel in front of him might be a terrifying abyss, but he held on to the idea of writing a single sentence. And after that, he'd write another true sentence. *Polay, polay.* One sentence at a time—with the faith that once he jumped, the story would be there.

After four years at the trauma center in upstate New York, my friend Kamal underwent a radical career change, crossing the continent and plunging into the venture capital world of Silicon Valley, where he became involved in some of the most exciting new start-ups in the heady early days of the Internet boom.

In the investment world, Kamal tells me, they talk about how a start-up is like jumping off a cliff and then building your plane while you're on the way down. Although he has a slightly different way of looking at it. "I prefer the image that on the way down, you sprout wings," he says. "It's been like that every time great things have happened in my life. I've jumped off cliffs, and I've fallen off sometimes, and to be honest, I've gotten bruises. But I'll tell you what, at least half the time you sprout wings. And it's the best feeling in the world."

One of the best expressions of this I've ever read comes from a Scottish mountaineer, William Murray, who served in the British army during World War II, was captured by the Germans in 1942, and spent the rest of the war years in prison camps. (Talk about an abyss.)

During his imprisonment, Murray began writing a book on his passion, which was mountain climbing. The only writing surface available to him was the camp's rough rag toilet paper. His manuscript was discovered and destroyed by the Gestapo. Murray was by this point so weak from the crap diet and poor conditions, he figured it was doubtful he would ever climb again. Still, he could write about it. To his fellow prisoners' amazement, he methodically stockpiled more toilet paper and started the damn book all over again, starting from page one.

The war finally came to an end, and in 1947 that second toilet-paper manuscript was published under the title *Mountaineering in Scotland*. Hailed as a masterpiece, it helped inspire a postwar renaissance in mountaineering. And he did climb again, too. In 1951 Murray was deputy leader to a Himalayan exploratory climb along with a certain gentleman by the name of Edmund Hillary. While he couldn't quite acclimate to the high altitude and thus could not join the team in its final climb, Murray's work helped pave the way for Hillary's historic 1953 summit of Mount Everest.

Some prisoners of war were crushed by the camp experience, their spirits totally broken; some died. Murray had a resolve that reached straight through his internment and up to the highest point on the planet. There is no force in the universe more powerful than a decided mind. In his 1951 book, *The Scottish Himalayan Expedition,* Murray penned a passage that has since become a hugely popular motivational quote:

Until one is committed, there is hesitancy, the chance to draw back, always ineffectiveness. Concerning all acts of initiative (and creation), there is one elementary truth, the ignorance of which kills countless ideas and splendid plans: that the moment one definitely commits oneself, then Providence moves too. All sorts of things occur to help one that would never otherwise have occurred. A whole stream of events issues from the decision, raising in one's favour all manner of unforeseen incidents and meetings and material assistance, which no man could have dreamt would have come his way.

When you make a clear, definitive decision, you gain access to resources that you would never have been able to tap otherwise. Courage is one; strength is another. So are the "unforeseen incidents and meetings and material assistance" Murray talks about.

How does this happen? I can't tell you. All I know is, it does.

Kamal says you sprout wings on the way down. As Murray showed, you sprout them on the way up, too.

DON'T LET ANYTHING STOP YOU

Sometimes when it comes time to jump, even though you may feel the universe giving you a nudge in the ass, the world around you may be shouting at you that you're wrong, you're not ready, you can't do it. Sometimes the world is right. Sometimes, though, it's wrong. That's a judgment call that only you can make.

How do you know? How do you know when the impulse to *go* really does mean the moment has arrived, and it's not just you being impulsive?

It's that trust-your-gut thing again. It's important to do your homework, to listen to the voice of experience, to get advice and guidance and wisdom from those who have gone before—but when the moment arrives, you can't look to the evidence to tell you if you should jump or not. You have to trust yourself. This, too, is like a set of muscles, and the only way to hone your jumping-off skills is to practice them.

Think back to the last time you were faced with a go-or-no choice, a fork in the road: jump or back off? What did you do? What were people around you telling you? With the benefit of hindsight, did you make the best choice? Every time you face a jump-or-stay choice, observe what happens, and evaluate carefully after the fact. Learn from your own experience, so that you come to rely more on your own gut than on the actions and opinions of those around you.

In May 1927 a young aviator named Charles Lindbergh made history by piloting his monoplane across the Atlantic. Lindbergh, of course, became an American hero, ticker tape parade in New York City, *Time* magazine's very first "person of the year," the whole nine thousand yards. He also inspired a young mechanic named Douglas Corrigan.

Douglas worked for the company that built Lindbergh's plane; in fact, he installed the fuel tanks and instrument panel and assembled the wings. He wanted to solo the Atlantic, too. Douglas was a first-generation American, and since his family had come over to the United States from Ireland, that would be his destination.

His plan did face a few problems, though. For example, he didn't have a plane. Or a pilot's license. Or any money. He got the license, started a business taking passengers up for rides, and eventually bought himself his own little monoplane. In 1935, he applied for permission to the Bureau of Air Commerce (predecessor of the FAA) for his proposed Ireland-bound trip. They said no, his plane wasn't up to it. He worked on the plane, applied again, got another no, then applied five more times and got turned down five more times.

He never did get a yes. But he didn't let that stop him.

In July 1938, Corrigan took off in a thick fog on a scheduled, approved flight from New York to California. Except that he flew in the other direction. And landed about twenty-eight hours later in Dublin. When flight officials questioned him, he told them he'd gotten mixed up in the fog, misread his compass, and simply flown the wrong way. They grilled him for a while, and he kept repeating the same answer. Finally he just shrugged and said, "That's my story."

When he returned to New York (by boat) he was greeted as a hero. The *New York Post* printed a giant headline saying, "HAIL TO WRONG WAY CORRIGAN!"—with the line of print running backward, right to left. He was celebrated with a ticker tape parade up Broadway with more than a million people lining the streets of Manhattan—a crowd several times larger than Lindbergh's.

The nickname "Wrong Way" Corrigan stuck with him for the rest of his life. To me, though, that misses the point. To me the point is not that he disobeyed the authorities and flew off in the opposite direction from his approved flight plan. It's that he was hell-bent on crossing the freaking Atlantic Ocean, and nothing was going to stop him from doing it. He stood on the cliff, heard all the reasons why he couldn't jump. And then jumped.

Lindbergh had financial backing, corporate resources, a brand-new plane in mint condition, and permission. Corrigan had none of those things. His plane was a wreck he'd picked up secondhand for a song, with an engine he cobbled together from two old Wright engines, and five extra fuel tanks that completely blocked his forward view. Some of the parts were held together with baling wire. During his cross-Atlantic flight his little plane developed a serious gas leak, which he "fixed" by punching a hole in the cockpit floor with a screwdriver to let the excess fuel drain into the ocean. And he crossed the freaking Atlantic.

Talk about a leap of faith.

Corrigan's story is a great illustration of *jumping off,* but I include it here for a personal reason, too. Recently my mom was digging into our genealogy and family history, and she discovered that her family, like so many others, immigrated to this country from Europe a century ago. Her great-grandmother's cousin was a guy name Corrigan.

Yes, *that* Corrigan.

Kamal says everyone has a superpower. "Brandon," he tells me, "yours is that you get shit done." I'd always assumed that came from my father, that ability to make a decision and then follow through come hell or high water. *We're going.* Turns out, it runs in my mom's side of the family, too.

CHOOSE LIFE

I've told you about my colossal business failure in 2011, and the dark place I found myself in its aftermath, and how I pulled myself out of that dark place. But there's something about that episode I didn't mention yet, and it might be the most significant element of that whole story. In the process, I learned something fascinating about failure. I came to see failure as quite different from the monster in the dark I'd been afraid of. Because that failure proved to be an experience worth millions.

In the course of building Wind Zero, I raised $3.8 million, diluted myself to 28 percent equity, learned how to leverage debt, learned about private equity groups and venture capital angels, negotiated the purchase of a thousand acres of real estate, put that real estate project through a complex entitlement process that took three years and required that I politick successfully with the local board of supervisors and other community leaders to get the whole thing approved. Yes, it eventually got scuttled and sunk. But man, what an education! That whole experience gave me a hard-core, school-of-hard-knocks MBA, including lessons I would never have learned in business school. As a result, I knew enough about how business works that if I lost everything tomorrow, I could go apply for an SBA loan the next day, buy a cash-flow-positive operation, and be back in business the day after that.

I also learned that fear of failure can in some ways be a

façade, a convenient excuse for what's really going on—and that what's really going on can be quite the opposite of what it seems. You don't do something because you're afraid of what might happen if you fail, and who could blame you for that? But you'd be amazed how often what seems like fear of failure is really fear of success hiding behind the camouflage.

Sure, what if you fail? *But what if you succeed?* What then?

I was afraid to write my first book, not because I thought it wouldn't sell but because I thought it would, and I didn't want to be judged. Guess what? It did, and I was. That's part of succeeding. It used to keep me up at night. It doesn't anymore. You just have to know that succeeding, like failing, comes with its own baggage. The more you deal with it, the better you get at it. Every triumph you bring with you, just like every failure, becomes a part of your tool kit for the next time around.

Theodore Roosevelt gave a speech once that I've already quoted in two other books (*The Killing School* and *Total Focus*), but it's worth quoting a third time:

> It is not the critic who counts; not the man who points out how the strong man stumbles, or where the doer of deeds could have done them better. The credit belongs to the man who is actually in the arena, whose face is marred by dust and sweat and blood; who strives valiantly; who errs, who comes up short again and again, because there is no effort without error and shortcoming; but who does actually strive to do the deeds; who knows

great enthusiasms, the great devotions; who spends himself in a worthy cause; who at the best knows in the end the triumph of high achievement, and who at the worst, if he fails, at least fails while daring greatly, so that his place shall never be with those cold and timid souls who neither know victory nor defeat.

A few years ago that quote was made popular to a whole new readership by social work research professor Brené Brown when she titled her bestselling book *Daring Greatly*. In that book, in direct homage to TR, she writes:

When we spend our lives waiting until we're perfect or bulletproof before we walk into the arena, we ultimately sacrifice relationships and opportunities that may not be recoverable, we squander our precious time, and we turn our backs on our gifts, those unique contributions that only we can make. *Perfect* and *bulletproof* are seductive, but they don't exist in the human experience.

A great number of common fears trace back to fear of the unfamiliar. That's what lurks behind a lot of prejudice and intolerance: hostility as an expression of fear. Fear of the different, the other, the unknown.

Just what *is* that?

I think fear of the unknown goes hand in hand with being attached to the known and the familiar, to being comfortable in your routine. Facing the unknown means you will probably have to adapt, which means to change. To grow.

In a word: to be *alive*.

In chapter 3 I suggested that many of our common fears are reflections of the fear of death. And yes, *You are going to die* is a terrifying thought, but here's what might be for some an even more terrifying thought: *Meanwhile, you're going to keep living.*

"The fear of death follows from the fear of life," said Mark Twain. "A man who lives fully is prepared to die at any time."

Fear of the unknown is huge. In the face of that kind of fear, there is a human instinct to invent a narrative that makes sense out of it all. So we invest time and energy in creating and telling ourselves stories that are probably not entirely true and are often limiting. We all know someone who, based purely on their abilities and talents, should be more accomplished than they are, but they've painted themselves as the victim of life and internalized it to the point that it becomes a self-fulfilling prophecy, the fabric of self-sabotage, mediocrity, and chronic underachievement. Afraid of success. Afraid of living.

Jumping off is an affirmation of living.

Really, jumping off *is* living.

PRACTICE POINTS

You can't reason or talk your way into this step. And you can't wait for the fear to go away, or until you feel 100 percent ready, because neither is ever going to happen. When the moment comes, it comes, and at that point it's about action, period. Preparation is logical, rational, and methodical. Jumping off is visceral.

Don't let anything stop you.

- Think back to the last time you made a bold decision, but then hesitated before taking action. Did you equivocate, second-guess yourself? How long did you stay in that place? Was it because you were still genuinely working through the decision, or were you simply hesitating for hesitation's sake?

- Think back to the last time you were faced with a risk your gut was telling you to take, but people around you were saying "Don't do it!" What did you do? With the benefit of hindsight, did you make the best choice? Sometimes the world is right, but sometimes it's wrong, and only you can decide.

- Resolve that the next time you find yourself in that hesitant gap between decision and action, you will cut the moment short—and simply act. If you are genuinely not sure and need more time to consider the decision, then step firmly back from the edge, climb down from the diving board, and take whatever steps you need to take in order to process the decision. But once you're as decided as you're going to be, then refuse to allow yourself the luxury of gratuitous hesitation. Just jump.

Make a habit of asking for what you want.

■ Whether it's a career advancement, a new position, assistance, or a favor, practice asking for what you want. Don't wait for the light to change from red to green. *Be* the green light.

■ You won't always get what you ask for; however:

- If you never make the request, your chances of getting it drop to near zero;

- Developing the habit of asking makes you a more decisive and action-oriented person;

- Making clear requests fosters good communication with others and also helps to clarify in your own mind what it is you want.

Have faith in the abyss.

- Find something you can trust, something you can hold on to in the face of the uncertainty of the jump. Trust in the strength, quality, and integrity of your preparation. Trust in the decision you've made. Trust your judgment. Trust in an outcome that serves the larger good.

- In the face of a task that seems overwhelming or insurmountable, find a manageable element that you *can* grasp—Hemingway's "one true sentence"—and execute that.

- When you are sure you can't go any further, take just one more step. And then just one more. *Polay, polay.*

5

KNOWING WHAT MATTERS

Lives remaining: Zero.

—ALEXIS OHANIAN,
cofounder of Reddit

S O LET'S SAY you've come this far. Like Kamal, you've *made the decision* to master fear and take this course of action, whatever it may be. To take on this challenge, confront this next level, open this new chapter in your life. You've agreed to come meet me at the pool every day, and we've spent a few days together.

You've *rehearsed.* You started out in your comfort zone, practiced the fundamental elements of the challenge, and gradually stretched the limits of your abilities, pushing yourself to the edge of your competence and beyond. You're as ready as you can be.

You've now *let go* of the wall, whatever wall it was that you were holding on to. And you're ready to *jump off*—to push out into the deep end and swim, to run to the edge and cannonball.

But you're not moving. Fear still holds you solidly in place, staring at the business card but not placing the call, standing stationary at the edge of the diving board, frozen on the precipice of action. What's missing?

Only the most important piece of the puzzle.

Earlier I said that the whole process of mastering fear starts with a decision. And that's true. Commitment doesn't come out of courage; it's the other way around. You make your decision, and the courage to see it through then arises out of that decision. But when you first read that back in chapter 1, there may have been a question nagging at the back of your mind: "How do I know which decision to make? If the courage to follow through comes out of the decision, what gives me the ability to make that decision in the first place?"

If you had that question, here's your answer: *knowing what matters.*

That's the key that unlocks the action at the tip of the diving board, that punches in the numbers on the keypad and presses SEND. The magic that sets your synapses firing and muscles engaging, that turns it all into the action that takes you all the way to the prize.

You might be tempted to think this step should really come first, before everything else, as chapter 1. And you wouldn't be wrong, because being clear on what matters *is* where the best decisions come from. Mastering fear starts with a decision; *knowing what matters* tells you which decision to make and gives you the strength to make it.

But I've saved this chapter for last for two reasons.

First, in practical reality that's often how it works. Often it's only in those moments of extreme duress, those times when we're staring an abyss in the face or confronting a challenge that seems insurmountable, that we suddenly find that crystal clarity: *This* is what matters—and nothing else really does. When people talk about going through a life-threatening crisis and say, "In an instant, my whole life flashed before my eyes," they aren't kidding. It's the brain doing an on-the-spot comprehensive file review: "If my life is about to end, I need to do an immediate replay of the entire damn thing so I know exactly what it is I'm fighting to hang on to."

I've also saved this step for last because it is the most important of the five, and I wanted it to stay with you long after you turn the last page and close the cover. Because here is the bottom line on fear: If you don't know what matters, fear will take over, pin you, and hold you down. If you're crystal clear on what matters, fear will propel you forward. It's really that simple.

The rest of it all helps: the decision, the rehearsal, the letting go. Learning to trust your gut. Listening to the voice of experience. Keeping the sharks out of your head. All of that is important. But this takes precedence. If you had to put your finger on a single focal point, a single strategy, a single action you could take to master your fear, it would be this: *Get clear on what matters.*

THE MOST IMPORTANT STEP

One day in early September 1996, Leo Russell decided to go for a swim.

Hurricane Edouard, the season's strongest storm, had just passed up the mid-Atlantic coast, doing far less damage than predicted. In Delaware, where Leo was vacationing with his family, the storm closed the beaches, but that was about it. In fact, Leo had just had a run during the storm and was now standing alone on Bethany Beach.

A swim would feel good.

Leo is not what you'd call a fitness nut, has never been in the military; he describes himself as "a normal guy who has lived a very ordinary life," at least in terms of physical challenges. Not that his childhood was 100 percent easy. His dad was an old-school, hard-drinking Irishman who married his Brazilian mother knowing he had cancer. A week past Leo's seventh birthday, Russell Sr. died. "That was a happy day for the Russell family," says Leo. The old man was one tough son of a bitch. Because of Leo's mother's iffy immigration status, the kids were taken away from her and put in foster care for a while. Once she managed to reclaim them, the family bounced around federal housing for six or seven years, then finally left the country. ("We were invited to leave," as Leo puts it.)

He spent the rest of his childhood in Brazil, going to an American school, then eventually repatriated, pursuing a career in business. Leo has a knack for sorting through things and solving problems, and he leveraged that gift to phenomenally successful effect. He ran venture capital for Lehman Brothers, served as CIO and EVP at Young & Rubicam, and founded Pride Global, one of the largest staffing companies in the world, where he continues today as CEO. I met him in New York. When I decided I wanted to up my game and take my media company from being a $100 million business to a $1 billion business, Leo was one of the guys I turned to.

Rough start notwithstanding, by Leo's account he has lived a blessed life. Super-successful in business, he has been happily married for forty years and has three wonderful kids. He's never been in combat, never been mugged or robbed, never even been picked on in the school playground. It's in *that* way, he clarifies, that he sees himself as entirely ordinary.

"You're a tough guy, Brandon," he tells me. "I'm your antiparticle. I am not a tough guy. I do not walk into a bar with pirates and take their booty away. I won't even go up in your plane." (It's true: I've tried. He refuses.) "I've never really experienced what you'd call deep fear, the kind where you literally fear for your life.

"Well," he adds, "except just the once."

This September day in 1996 was the once.

Standing on that Delaware beach, Leo looked around. The worst of the weather was long past. He strode into the surf and launched himself into the water, bodysurfing along the coast. It felt great . . . until it didn't. Suddenly the surf surged under him. A great wave picked Leo up and flipped him over, slamming him against a rock outcropping and crushing his right leg—a compound fracture, as he would later learn, that took about an inch of bone off his leg.

In an instant, Leo was crippled. And alone. There was no one else on the beach for miles.

In a moment like this, your physiology faces an abrupt choice, a neurological and endocrine fork in the road: PANIC or CALM? The natural response is to panic, to let adrenaline have its way with you and plunge full bore into thrash-and-struggle mode. Typically, in a situation such as this, that is exactly the response that leads to a rapid and quite unpleasant death.

Leo felt himself slipping into panic.

And then a single thought shot through him, quick as a bolt of lightning and just as electric. In an instant, all his mental and physiological reponses switched over from PANIC to CALM.

All at once, he found himself able to assess the situation. There was no way he could beat the force of the undertow. He saw that if he kept flailing and trying to swim through the waves toward shore, he would just be carried farther out. However, he reasoned, if he let himself sink all the way down to the bottom, and grabbed enough vegetation to anchor himself to the ocean floor, he might be far enough under the current to where he could pull himself along toward shore. He implemented the plan: he let himself sink, grabbed what flora he could, and began moving. He had to surface at intervals for air, but each time, he let himself sink again and managed to crawl back under the waves, digging in whenever the current got stronger and then inching forward when the force receded. Eventually he made it to shore.

So here's what I wanted to know: How the hell did he pull that off?

No doubt, part of it was Leo's long training in sitting with a problem and dispassionately deconstructing it. That's the *rehearsal* part. But a well-trained methodical mindset doesn't explain it, not fully, because up to this point in his life he'd had zero experience in facing or responding to any kind of life-threatening circumstance. None of his training in business had prepared him for a physically grueling situation like this. So what got him through? What was that single thought that flashed through his mind, instantly resetting all his switches from PANIC to CALM?

It was this: his wife and their three-week-old son, at the house where the family was staying a few miles away.

"I had kind of a crazy upbringing myself," says Leo. "I compensate for it by trying to be the best husband and father

I can be. And I *had* to show up for my kid's first birthday."
That was the lightning bolt that shot through his nervous
system and switched him from a panicked response that would
have spelled his death to the measured response that saved
his life.

I have to be there.

Leo didn't need to think about it. He didn't have to make
up a list of core values and then weigh and sort and rank
them. This wasn't a conceptual thing. It was bone-deep and
instantaneous. There was nothing more important than being at his son's first birthday. *Nothing.*

The fear was so strong it nearly paralyzed him. The drive
to see his son again was stronger.

And that's how it is for you, for me, and for every one of
us. We all experience fear—but for every single one of us
there is also something in our lives that is stronger, that matters more, that will *always* win out and carry the day.

We just have to know what it is.

KEEP MONEY IN PERSPECTIVE

Last year my friend James did something unexpected. Which,
James being James, should have caught nobody by surprise,
but it did. He got rid of all his stuff. I mean, everything. He
hung on to a few outfits (pants, shirts, shoes), and a laptop
and a phone. That's pretty much it. This is a guy who has

pocketed a not-so-small fortune through his investments, businesses, books, and other activities. A multimillionaire many times over.

And did I mention homeless? Technically speaking, anyway. James doesn't have a house or apartment of his own. Instead, he lives in Airbnbs, here and there. Now he's sort of a brilliant, nerdy, Jewish, multimillionaire Jack Reacher (without the violence).

James says, "I got rid of everything but my laptop and my curiosity." Wondering how things work, learning new knowledge, and sharing what he learns with as many others as possible to help make their lives better: for James, on the list of what's important, that's right at the top.

I told you in chapter 3 about my friend Maria and the immense hurdles she faced getting her EmbroidMe business off the ground in 2008. Fast-forward seven years: by 2015 the business had become phenomenally successful, with every major design house, name brand, and star-power celebrity you can think of beating a path to her door in Manhattan.

But now she faced a new dilemma. As much as she loved her business, it wasn't her true passion. The whole time, she'd had a project going on the side, creating on-site events at stores where she would interact with customers to create their own custom designs right there on the spot. She loved the energy of it.

One day she was talking to me about the stress of juggling them both, her hugely successful retail storefront and her traveling pet project. I stopped her, then asked her to look me right in the eyes and explain her EmbroidMe business in a few sentences. Then I asked her to do the same with her on-site project. The transformation, from the first Maria to the second, was dramatic.

"You see that?" I said when she paused for breath. "You see how different you were when you described each one? Your voice, your facial expressions? It was like you were two different people!"

She saw, all right. It was impossible not to.

"So tell me," I said. "Which would you like to be doing every day?"

"Wait," she said. "What are you talking about? I can't just stop the store—I'm *obligated*. I can't just give it up!"

Sure she could. I knew it sounded crazy. But when she described her on-site work, she positively glowed. "That passion, that level of excitement?" I told her. "Hell, *I'd* want to be around that. Anyone would. *That's* what you need to be doing. Do the thing that makes you feel alive." I encouraged her to take this thing she'd been doing on the side for years to support her "real" business and make a brand out of it.

So she did. She put her business up for sale and began getting some decent offers, but they all included clauses that would have kept Maria on, running the business for the new owners for years, which was the opposite of what she wanted. She couldn't find the right buyer or the right deal. Finally she decided she had to get her ego out of the picture; she had to stop fixating on the number she wanted and just let go of the business.

She gave her business to a new owner.

I don't mean she sold it. I mean *gave*. As in, for the total purchase price of zero. A highly successful, thriving, multi-million-dollar Manhattan business. *And she gave it away*. The money, the ego, the ownership—none of that mattered, compared with the feeling Maria got from working directly with people one-on-one in her on-site work. Maria got clear on what was important.

I was sitting next to her the day she designed her new company's website. I've never seen her happier.

Don't get me wrong. The moral of this story is not "Money doesn't matter." Of course it matters. It matters a lot. I'm sure you've heard this one: "Money can't buy happiness." Biggest crock ever. Money can put good food on the table, buy your kids clothes, pay for a great trip you can take together, buy you a better home that's safer and more comfortable and more enjoyable to wake up to every day, maybe in a city you love, or in the countryside you love, or someplace with mountains, or the ocean, or a lake. Money can buy you tickets to a fantastic show. Money can pay for the surgery your cousin needs, or your father, or your kid, or a friend. Money can pay for art lessons, skydiving lessons, a museum tour of Europe, a ski trip on the back of Mont Blanc.

Money can't buy happiness? Bullshit! Money can buy a *ton* of happiness. But only if you already know what's important. What money *can't* do is figure that out for you.

DON'T LET THE GLITTER DISTRACT YOU

Money is not the only thing that can distract you from what really matters. There are all sorts of things in your world that can do that.

When Kamal moved to Silicon Valley early in his career, he knew essentially nothing about the tech business or high-stakes investment. He just showed up and jumped off that particular cliff. His timing was excellent. He found a start-up to join and helped build that company, which ended up going public and doing very well. (In fact, it is one of the few from those early dot-com days that's still around.) That success established his reputation. He began consulting for CEOs of big companies, and started a few himself. Some did better than others, but all in all, his career was plowing along beautifully.

"I thought I was having success," he says. "In all honesty, though, there was a lot of ego there."

Then he started the company that was going to be The Big One. He figured this would be his last hurrah, the one that would set him up for life. He wasn't just going to make money, he was going to make buy-your-own-island money. "What in Silicon Valley they call fuck-you money," he says, "meaning, *I've got so much money I can do whatever the hell I want*. Which is all ego, by the way."

Rather than take any outside investment, he built this company from scratch himself, funding it himself, pouring into it everything he had. It took off and grew like crazy, and that made him want to build it even bigger, so now investors began jumping in, and now things *really* started to take off.

You probably see where this is heading.

In the beginning, Kamal would motivate his team by telling them about how they were going to transform their industry, and about the incredible difference they were going to make together. Over time, that changed. Soon he was motivating them by telling them about how much money they were all going to make. A different vision translates into different priorities, which yield different decisions. You choose different partners. Take different critical actions.

And of course, the thing blew up. It blew up hard and messy.

"And because my ego was so attached to it," says Kamal, "when it blew up, I blew up with it." The total collapse of the business precipitated a crisis that plunged Kamal into the depths of illness and near-suicidal despair, which in turn eventually led to his resurrection through the process he describes in his little book *Love Yourself Like Your Life Depends on It*.

Here's what came out of that collapse: a new clarity about what matters.

Looking back at that colossal meltdown, Kamal realized that the whole time he was building his company, he was attached to the outcome. He was attached to the singular goal of *that company succeeding.* But that wasn't what mattered. He was aiming at the wrong target. What mattered was not what he was achieving, but who he was becoming in the process. All the rest—the sense of accomplishment, the accolades, the power, the prestige, and yes, the money—all that was just glitter.

Most of us will never go through the experience of creating a multimillion-dollar Silicon Valley start-up. But we've all had the experience of reaping different kinds of rewards for our efforts, whether large or small. Praise from others. A financial windfall. A rush of pride, thrill of accomplishment. A title, a promotion. The look on other people's faces when they are impressed with what you've done.

None of that is bad. But it's all glitter. It's all wrapping paper and ribbons, not what's inside the box.

What's inside the box is who you are becoming in the process.

"One of the keys to a rich life is to understand that we are the *effort,*" says Kamal. "We're never the outcome. And it's ironic, because if you focus on the effort, on who you are, on expressing yourself and putting that out to the world, the outcome will be far better than anything you could have planned for. Really. Guaranteed."

DON'T LET THE SUFFERING DISTRACT YOU, EITHER

Sometimes moments of extreme duress can clarify what matters, as that moment in 1996 did for Leo Russell. Sometimes, though, the stress of adversity can feel so brutal, so difficult, so soul-crushing that it threatens to make you feel like just giving up, giving in, letting go of what matters, and settling for whatever shreds and remnants of life you can salvage. Or not even that. In the United States, there are well over a hundred deaths by suicide every day—more than forty thousand a year. And there are tens of thousands more people who keep walking and breathing but have already given up on living.

It's easy to be distracted by the glitter of fame and fortune. It's just as easy to have your personal vision blinkered by the pain of everyday existence—and especially by those moments when that pain rises to levels that feel intolerable.

I recently went to a YPO meeting to hear a talk given by Nando Parrado, cofounder of the Uruguayan chapter of YPO. I've heard a lot of stories of hardship and suffering, but this one topped them all. It was one of the best talks I've ever heard.

Nando was a college student in Uruguay who played on his school's rugby team. In 1972, as he and his team were flying a chartered turboprop over the Andes on their way to

Chile for a match, their plane clipped a mountaintop and ripped in half. The back portion of the plane was severed, killing everyone inside instantly, including Nando's mother, who was traveling with them. The front of the plane bounced over one mountain peak, launched like a skipping stone, then over another, landing on the downslope and skidding down a steep incline before coming to a stop.

"One moment," said Nando, "you're joking with your teammates, these kids you've grown up with, kids you've known all your life. Everything is happy. And suddenly, in a millisecond, it's not." It reminded me of Kamal, talking about his experience in the ER, seeing all those people who'd been suddenly brought face-to-face with the fact that safety is an illusion.

These kids had never been in snow, never seen snow. They were wearing their street clothes. Now they were stranded somewhere deep in the Andes at nearly twelve thousand feet. Night came, with freezing high-mountain temperatures. Then another day, and a night, and then another, and another. On day eight Nando's sister died; by this time only twenty-seven of the original forty-eight people on the plane were still alive. On day eleven they found a transistor radio among the wreckage and learned that the search effort to find the downed plane had been called off, the entire party presumed dead. On day seventeen an avalanche hit, killing eight more.

The story went on, and just got worse and worse. The surviving group began starving to death and were eventually forced to resort to cannibalizing their departed friends in order to stay alive. After two months—*two months*—Nando and his friend Roberto Canessa took off and hiked what turned out to be more than a hundred miles before they eventually found help. They were rescued on day seventy; the rescue effort reached the others within the next two days.

Nando talked about the the fear of freezing to death, of starving to death, of dying alone. "When you are young," he said, "you feel immortal." Suddenly that illusion was ripped away. Everything had lost its meaning, and the only thing left in its place was fear.

After he returned to Uruguay and had fully recovered physically, he found those fears all still haunted him. He was home and safe, and to all appearances the horrific event was behind him—but it still had him paralyzed with fear. He was alive, but not living. Finally one day his father said, "Nando, you cannot let this define you. You have to look at this experience as a rebirth. You've been given a new life. Now you have to go out and live it."

So he did. He threw himself into life as if he had never lived it before. He'd always wanted to race cars; now he became a professional race car driver. He fell in love, got married, gave up racing cars. Started businesses, became a television personality, built a $100 million empire. None of it took away his fear. Over time, though, all these experiences, both the suffering and the glitter, put dying—and living—into a different perspective.

"The next time I find myself dying," he said, "I know what I will remember. Not my fast cars and businesses, contracts and bank loans and earnings, emails and airports. I like a Ferrari, a nice dinner, the good things in life. But none of it matters. The warmth of my daughters' embrace at night when I put them to bed, or the quiet presence of my wife, Veronique, near me: These are moments that will not be repeated. These moments are what is important."

Ever since the dawn of storytelling people have asked the question: Why do bad things happen to good people? Scholars say the story of Job is one of the oldest in the Bible. Why does a kid like Nando end up at twelve thousand feet of snow in sneakers, losing his mother and sister and a bunch of his friends and experiencing a horror most of us can't even imagine?

Why do terrible things happen to good people? I don't know. But maybe it happens, in part, to do for people what it did for Nando: to clarify what matters.

Hearing Nando's story reminded me of *Man's Search for Meaning*, Viktor Frankl's story of survival in a concentration camp in Nazi Germany, one of the most influential books of the twentieth century. If you asked me to choose a single book about how to develop yourself as a human being, how to grow your character and live a richer life, Frankl's would be my hands-down choice. Few have chronicled a story of greater hardship or more extreme suffering than this one.

The conclusions he comes away with are fascinating. He talks about the greatest struggles that face the survivors of catastrophe (which he names as bitterness and disillusion- ment) and about the salvation that arrives, without fanfare, wrapped inside each moment of love, decency, and compan- ionship.

Every one of us experiences loss. I know I have. And I know you have, too. Few of us will ever know suffering on the level of a Nando Parrado or a Viktor Frankl. Still, loss is loss.

Maybe you experienced loss of a friendship when some- one you trusted betrayed you, or when you were young and a friend's family moved away. Or perhaps you had a great ath- letic career ahead of you, but you tore your knee in college and had to go into some other field. You lost a lot of money. A business went south. A buddy went down the drug rabbit hole and never came back. A parent died way too early. Or you had a child who died. Or your own childhood was a horror story, and you never got to enjoy the kinds of early bonding experi- ences you've heard others reminisce about. Whatever it was, you've felt the pain of loss. Hey, it goes with the territory of humanity.

There are two ways to go here. The loss can break you, or it can deepen you. It can make you bitter about what you don't have. Or it can make you more deeply appreciate what you do have. It can clarify what matters.

TREAT EACH HOUR LIKE IT'S WORTH MORE THAN GOLD

After hearing Nando speak I went back home to my place in New York and sat, thinking about what he said. I needed to hear that talk. Now I found myself asking, "What am I doing?" Over the years since my marriage ended, I'd been in several serious relationships with amazing women. Yet I'd broken off each one, and for the last few years I'd been dating a series of younger women, knowing it wasn't serious and wasn't ever going to get serious. I had to stop and ask: What's important here? I should be looking at dating with an eye toward creating a real, long-term relationship.

Really, there was no time to waste. I'd forgotten that. Nando reminded me.

Nando learned something at age nineteen that has taken me quite a few more years to learn: the value of time.

In the middle of 2012, after my first book came out, I started work on another book, a memoir about a handful of SEALs I'd known and worked with who gave the ultimate sacrifice. The idea for the book was inspired by Michael Bearden Sr., father of the Bear, the friend I described in chapter 4 who perished in a jump exercise. I started a draft, and I was in the midst of writing that September when I got the news that my best and closest friend in the world, Glen Doherty, had been killed in the attack in Benghazi.

All of a sudden, the book I was writing was about my best friend.

Up till that moment I'd fully expected to be hanging out with Glen well into old age. I'd always assumed that it would *always* be Glen and me, going surfing, going flying, having crazy adventures together, sitting around talking from midnight till dawn, staying in touch and helping each other in our careers and looking out for each other in our lives. We would be best friends in our seventies. Hell, maybe our eighties. Why not?

And suddenly, it was all past tense. We wouldn't spend decades hanging out; we wouldn't spend even another two minutes hanging out. It was over.

The moment you're born, the hand of time starts swinging, like a sword of Damocles suspended over your head by a single hair, and you don't know when it's going to fall. Because there are only two things we know for sure. We know that we're alive, right here, right now. And we know that at some point, that's going to end. What we don't know is everything else.

You cannot afford to waste a single hour.

And I'm not talking about efficiency, or about being organized or productive. When I say "you cannot afford to waste a single hour," what I mean is this: to gain mastery of your life, you need to treat each hour as if it's the only one you have left.

That was the conversation I had that day with my friend

Maria, when she was talking about the challenge of juggling two different businesses. "Why are you making yourself miserable? Go do what makes you happy!"

I told you about the courage it took my friend C.J. to take the stage and play with the Ramones, but I also need to tell you about the courage it took him *not* to take the stage more than a decade later.

In 2001, five years after the Ramones had folded, C.J. had the chance to take over the vacant bass player position in the iconic band Metallica. His place in rock-and-roll history had already been solidly established, but for all their critical success, the Ramones never had the kind of box office success that some other bands had. Bands like Metallica. Taking that position would have sent C.J.'s career into the stratosphere. But there was a problem. C.J.'s son had autism, and he felt it was important to have his time free to be there every day with the family, supporting their child. He turned the position down.

"I was honored that they asked me," he says, "but there was just no way I could do it."

Digital entrepreneur Alexis Ohanian, whom *Forbes* magazine dubbed "the mayor of the Internet," says that Reddit, the company he cofounded, dominated his life for the first sixteen months they were in full start-up mode. This is a guy who knows how to go nonstop full tilt as well as anyone in the world. Coming out of that experience, he decided he would never again let one project overtake his life to the exclusion of everything else that mattered.

"I always encourage founders that I've invested in or advise that they take some time to appreciate the fact that they've only got one shot at this," he said in an interview in *Wired*. "You have to live your life as if it were a video game, and at the top of the screen it says, 'Lives remaining: Zero.'"

WHAT MATTERS TO ME

In the fall of 2017, while we were working on this manuscript, Hurricane Maria ripped through the Caribbean and devastated Puerto Rico, where I live. (I have an apartment in Manhattan, but my Puerto Rico place is home.) Friends checked in with me to sympathize and find out how my place survived the storm, and were surprised when I answered, "There's nothing down there that couldn't wash away that I would care about."

It's not really that I don't *care* about any of it. Of course I do. I have personal things there, memorabilia, artifacts from the journey that has been my life so far. If I didn't care about that stuff, I wouldn't have it in my place. But it doesn't really matter. My family's not there. The whole building could wash into the sea and I'd be fine. It's just stuff.

A catastrophe like a Category 5 hurricane, or an earthquake, or a war, or an economic collapse is a horrifying thing. It can also be a clarifying thing, because it takes away everything you have. When you strip away all the material things, it throws your life into a harsh but brutally honest light. There is no more dancing around the point or ignoring what lies at the heart of it all. My goal is to remember that at all times, without needing the catastrophe to point it out.

So here, in no particular order, is what matters to me:

ETHICS

Creating an online space for honoring our Spec Ops vets was the impulse that created Hurricane. A site where we could shine the light on stolen valor (people pretending to be Spec Ops vets who are not), corruption at the VA, and other issues that affect the military and veteran community. Strong ethics is a big part of what drives the men and women in uniform, and it drives me still today.

TRUTH

Another primal factor in the genesis of Hurricane Media. There is way too much slant, subjectivity, distortion, and flat-out inaccuracy in the mainstream media. We may not be the slickest or smoothest news site out there, we may not always have the most perfect syntax or polished language, but we always tell the truth. Honesty and integrity are the core language of our operating system.

EXCELLENCE

For me, part of appreciating the value of time means I don't want to waste a moment of effort on anything less than excellence. Wanting to be part of an elite team that aspired to be the best in the world was the number one factor that drove me to join the SEALs in the first place.

FREEDOM

For all the criticism you can levy against the state of our country—and much of it is justified, because there is so much that is a mess right now—all of that mess and negativity pales in comparison to the qualities that make this country great. I am a confirmed skeptic, but not a cynic (there's a difference), and I believe in the greatness of the United States with all my heart. Plenty of other countries around the world enjoy varying levels of freedom, but in all my travels, I've never encountered a culture that has the love of freedom so deeply embedded in its DNA as this one.

MY FRIENDS, MY TEAM

There is an incredibly strong team ethic in the Spec Ops world. Yes, we're fighting for our country and for democracy and all that good stuff. But when you're actually there, trudging on for miles in the dirt or the sand or the snow, with the electric buzz of mortal danger humming in the air, or when guns and bombs start going off and the whole place suddenly fills with smoke and chaos, you are not thinking about flag and freedom; you are thinking about keeping the guy next to you alive.

I've brought that same sense of team to my business. I don't look at them as employees; I consider them family. As I write, our team comprises more than fifty people, distributed geographically all over the globe. Two years ago, I would talk with everyone on staff in the course of a normal week, but this year I realized we'd grown to the point where that could no longer happen. I had to start writing a newsletter to the team. But I didn't want it just to be them hearing from me. I wanted it to be a genuine communication, not just a now-hear-this set of announcements from the captain. So here's how I do that: I have everyone on our staff send me an email every month, telling me what's important to them, both personally and professionally, along with what their biggest challenge is. After I read through all those responses, *then* I put together that month's newsletter. It helps keep us connected.

A few years ago I started holding an annual meeting, flying everyone in from around the world to spend a few days together. Now I've upped that to twice a year. Yes, I want to grow my business from $100 million to $1 billion. But that's only one metric. There's no more core measure of our company's success than the success of everyone on the team.

MY FAMILY

My three children are the fuel that drives my desire to succeed. Everything I build, whether it's a company or a book or a foundation or a circle of friends, I approach first and foremost as the building of a legacy that they can look up to and be proud of.

This book is about fear, so I'll share what is my biggest fear these days: that I will fail to provide everything I could for my three children to have a stable and happy future. I don't mean in the form of a cash handout; I mean the full balance of life lessons I can impart and experiences I can share through our many adventures together and our conversations together about life and career.

As I write, all three are in their teens, and that bank account of shared experiences has built up a pretty solid balance. I know we won't have forever to do that, but it feels like we're almost there.

THAT'S MY LIST: ethics, truth, excellence, freedom, friends, team, family. If a hurricane blows in tomorrow and takes away everything I own—my apartments, my planes, my business, my bank accounts, my gun collection, my art, my books, my clothes, my shoes—as long as I still have what's on that list, I'm good.

WHAT MATTERS TO YOU?

That's what matters to me, but I'm just me. I imagine it's different for everyone. Sure, there are common themes, values a lot of us tend to share. Family, friends, freedom, those are pretty universal things. But really knowing what matters most? That's an individual journey.

So that prompts the question: What matters to you?

It's not a rhetorical question. In fact, I suggest you put this book down, take out a notebook or your iPad or whatever you use to write on, and respond to that question with some concrete answers. Go ahead. Start a list.

What really matters to you?

I don't know if that list will have three items on it or ten. Or one. This is your life, not mine. Just start the list. What matters? Abstract answers are fine here—to start with. But no fear was ever mastered, no opponent beaten back, no hardship grappled with or major challenge met head-on, with nothing but an abstraction in hand to inspire the struggle. If the only thing on Leo Russell's mind was "Family—yeah, I like the sound of that: *family* . . ."—then he would have drowned off the coast of Delaware right then and there.

No. The thought that arced through Leo's brain wasn't "family"; it was *I have to see my son again.*

So once you've written down those abstract answers, then go back and get concrete about it. Freedom, great, but what do you mean by that? Family—fine, but who, exactly? What about them?

And by the way, it's totally okay if you stare at the pad and it stays blank. That's fantastic, actually, because it means you're being honest. Maybe you really don't know the answers. Or not yet. Sometimes you don't realize what really matters until you're faced with one of those clarifying moments—the car crash, the surgeon's pronouncement, the house fire. Sometimes I wonder if you *did* know, if you did take the time and quiet, honest self-reflection to dig deep for those answers, maybe the car crash and the house fire and all the rest wouldn't be necessary at all.

Of course, that's just speculation. I don't pretend to know how these things work, this machinery of life and circumstance. But I do know this: everything you really want is on the other side of fear.

I can't tell you what it is, or what it looks like, or where to find it. But I can offer this clue: *start with what you fear.* And don't suppress it, or fight it, or try to put it behind you—embrace it. Make it your ally. Trust it. Master it.

It will point you in the direction of what matters most.

PRACTICE POINTS

Mastering fear starts with a decision, but it is knowing what matters that tells you which decision to make and leads you to make it in the first place. There has to be something important—that is, important *to you*—that makes the risk worth it. Here is the bottom line on fear: If you don't know what matters, fear will hold you back. If you're crystal clear on what matters, fear will propel you forward.

Identify what matters most.

■ Make a list of everything that is most important to you. Don't worry about what order the entries are in, or about the list being complete. You can come back and add to it later. Just get it down.

■ Now go back over that list and make each item concrete and specific. If you wrote down a value, such as "freedom," "truth," "contribution," or "success," what specifically does that mean? If you wrote down something about people, such as "friends" or "family" or "relationships," then who? And what about them?

■ Go through it once more, and this time ask yourself these questions about each entry on your list:

- How much time am I devoting to this each week?

- How much of the money I earn am I investing in this?

- How much of my energy am I investing in this every day?

- If I knew I had one year left to live, would I change any of those three answers above?

- How, exactly?

- How can I start implementing those changes right now?

CONCLUSION

SOLO FLIGHT

*I have never in my life envied a human being
who led an easy life. I have envied a great many
people who led difficult lives and led them well.*

—THEODORE ROOSEVELT

ONE CHILLY DAY in early 2004, in the middle of an old
military airfield right on the San Diego–Tijuana border,
my flight instructor, John Carey, pulled a surprise. We were
taxiing along the runway when John's gravelly voice suddenly spoke up: "Hey, pull over. This is where I hop out.
You're gonna solo this thing."

I had no idea this was coming. He hadn't given me a clue.
Though I didn't know it at the time, this is an old-school military aviation tradition: you don't know when you're going to
do your first solo, and your flight instructor springs it on you.
To be honest, I was kind of floored. Was I ready for this? But
there was no point in even asking the question. What was I
going to do, say no?

"Okay," I said.

I pulled over. He hopped out. I accelerated again, pulled back on the stick, and took off. It was an exhilarating feeling—scary, but at the same time, such a rush. And not just the thrill of flying but that flush of new confidence: *Oh, I can do this!*

I did three or four laps around the pattern by myself, and that was it. I was hooked.

In a small plane you don't have the hydraulics that run the big airplanes; a lot of it is purely mechanical. When you pull back on the stick for takeoff, you're feeling the actual mechanical resistance of all that wind and air pressure you're pulling against. We call it *stick and rudder,* where you feel the control services, feel the connection between man, machine, and the elements. I love everything about it. There's a little trim wheel that trims the elevator, which neutralizes some of that resistance. If you find you're having to pull back really hard, you can trim the elevator, which takes some of that control pressure out of the yoke. John calls it "the pilot's best friend." Even today, all these years later, whenever I fly I still hear his voice in my ear, yelling, "Goddamn it, trim the plane! Trim the damn plane!"

After you do that first short solo, they send you out on what they call a cross-country flight: a hundred miles or more, far enough that you encounter different wind currents, changes in cloud cover, maybe weather changes, changing conditions you have to adapt to all on your own. First you do it as a dual cross-country, which you plan yourself but then fly with your instructor. The next day you fly it alone. My cross-country solo was from San Diego to Santa Barbara. About two hundred miles. It wasn't that challenging, technically speaking—but it was one of the most intense flying experiences I've ever had.

Because I was piloting the thing *myself.*

The whole way, I heard John's cracked, weathered old voice in my head. *Brandon? Please trim the plane before you kill us. Trim the damn plane! Thank you.*

Starting my business was exactly like that. One chilly day in early 2012, sketching out a basic website design on the back of a napkin and making the decision to leave my high-paying executive job and stake my future on that napkin. Once you know what it's like to be the captain of your own destiny, you never want to go back. Flying your own plane, captaining your own ship, running your own business—they're all really the same thing. Making the decisions to get from point A to point B, there's a ton of responsibility—and I love it. It's the most amazing feeling. There's this sense of *agency,* this high you get from knowing that, by your wits and thoughts and actions alone, *you* are making this impossible thing happen.

And I do mean *you.* Because, while you may not be a pilot, or a sea captain, or an entrepreneur, or a CEO, that doesn't matter. Those are just details. You're still the one in charge of your own time, your own life and legacy.

They say that when all is said and done, what matters is the love in your life, the relationships, the people you make the journey with. I believe that. My kids, my close friend-ships? There's nothing more important to me.

Still, that doesn't change the reality.

The reality is, your life is up to you. No one else. Every one of us comes into this life alone, and alone we go out again. Your life is defined by a series of choices, and the one who makes every one of those decisions is purely and solely *you*. Yes, you have friends, advisers, mentors, colleagues, teammates; you love and are loved by others. Any of us who've been in the armed forces know that we would willingly put our lives on the line for our brothers and sisters, give our lives to save theirs. All that is true, and none of that changes the fact that you are the one running your race, and no one else can run it for you, not even one step.

Life is a solo flight. You are the captain. And it's not a 747, with all the hydraulics and fancy equipment and massive automation. It may seem like it sometimes, like you can switch things onto automatic pilot and sit back and relax, maybe even catch a few minutes of the in-flight movie. But trust me, it's a tiny, single-engine craft, no hydraulics, all mechanicals, where you feel the resistance of air pressure pulling against the strength of your arms and shoulders.

It's all stick and rudder.

And while love and friendship may be the fuel, *fear* is your navigator. Not your adversary, but your copilot, its cracked, weathered voice in your ear, saying, *Please trim the plane before you kill us. Trim the damn plane! Thank you.*

This is where I hop out.

You're soloing this thing.

ACKNOWLEDGMENTS

Writing a book feels like jumping out of a plane when you start, and scaling a mountain by the time you're finished. When you summit and turn around to take in the view, the first thing you see is the skilled and dedicated team that helped you get there. My thanks and appreciation go out:

To my writing partner, the talented and versatile John David Mann; this is our sixth outing together, and I couldn't ask for a better dive buddy or climbing partner.

To our phenomenal team at Portfolio/Penguin: Bria Sandford, Helen Healey, Alison Coolidge, Tara Gilbride, Will Weisser, and Adrian Zackheim; you guys are as pro as it gets, and it's always a pleasure working with you.

To Alyssa Reuben and Katelyn Dougherty at the Paradigm Talent Agency, for helping keep everything on track.

To all the brave men and women, known to me personally or by reputation only, whose stories of mastering fear appear in these pages: James Altucher, Neil Amonson, Lanny Bassham, Mike Bearden Jr. (aka the Bear), Douglas Corrigan, Maria Emma, Viktor Frankl, Chief Dan Goulart, William H. Murray, Alexis Ohanian, Nando Parrado, James Powell, C. J. Ramone, Leo Russell, Ernest Shackleton, Curtis Thornhill, José Torres, Captain Jerry Yellin.

To the friends and mentors who have been part of the encounters with fear described herein: Kennedy, our H-60 copilot; Captain Mike Roach, of the dive boat *The Peace;* John Carey, my aviation instructor; my BUD/S teammate and training partner Eric Davis; and my best friend, Glen Doherty.

To all my amazing guests on my *Power of Thought* podcast.

To all my courageous passengers who've allowed me to fly them over the Manhattan skies and other spots around the globe; and to all my flight instructors, domestic and foreign.

To my dad, Jack; my mom, Lynn; my grandmother Doris; and Grandma Barb and Grandpa Jack, for their examples of courage, strength, and perseverance.

To my three children; you are a constant inspiration and the fuel that keeps my plane in the air.

Finally to my best friend, Kamal Ravikant, who told me to write this book, and whose presence and wisdom hover over every page.

INDEX

INDEX